Real Life University

Mastering the Maze

Real Life University

Mastering the Maze

BY

Nicole Amare

AND

Michael McMyne

PREMIUM PRESS AMERICA
NASHVILLE, TENNESSEE

REAL LIFE UNIVERSITY Mastering the Maze
by Michael McMyne and Nicole Amare

Published by PREMIUM PRESS AMERICA

ISBN 1-887654-47-X

Library of Congress Catalog Card Number: 2002091252

PREMIUM PRESS AMERICA books are available at special discounts for premiums, sales promotions, fund-raising, or mechanical use. For details contact the Publisher at P.O. Box 159015, Nashville TN 37215, or call toll-free 800/891-7323 or 615/256-8484, or fax 615/256-8624.

For more information visit our web site at www.premiumpress.com.

Edit and Layout by Armour&Armour, Nashville, Tennessee
Cover by Bob Bubnis/BookSetters, Nashville, Tennessee

First Edition 2002
1 2 3 4 5 6 7 8 9 10

*We dedicate this book
to our loving parents,*

Bob and Yvette McMyne
and
Paul and Fran Ervin,

*who inspire us through their
generosity, selflessness, and love.*

ACKNOWLEDGMENTS

We have been blessed to have so many hard-working members on our team who have contributed a great deal to the success of this project. Through the tireless efforts of the following people, *Real Life University* has finally become a reality:

First is our publisher, George Schnitzer, for being such a strong believer in our project and working diligently to ensure its success. Through his optimism, energy, dedication, and professionalism, we are able to help future university students all over the country.

We are deeply grateful for Michael McCrossen for introducing Michael to the speaking profession and for being the inspiration behind McMyne & Associates. His genius has taught us a lot. Without his daily support and tenacious attitude, this book would have never begun.

Special thanks to Francis Bologna, who encouraged us to begin this manuscript, and whose inspiration fills these pages.

We wish to recognize Gary Conner for his enthusiasm, flexibility, and his willingness to always be there when we needed his assistance and expertise.

Extraordinary gratitude goes to Mary Whittington; if every university in America had a Mary, things would be a little brighter in college education today.

We are eternally appreciative for Gary Conner, Margaret Feeney, Erin Gallagher, Neil Hatchard, Doug James, Susan Kocour, Andrew Lauber, Alan Manning, Melanie McMyne, Dominic O'Keffe, Megan Overstreet, and Todd Ramsey for reading and openly responding to various drafts of this book.

Not only are we grateful for those who have had a direct impact on this book, but we also wish to recognize those who have touched our lives in a special way:

We thank Dr. Tom Nuttli for using his innate strength in the field of medicine to all but heal Michael from the sickness that plagued his life for so many years.

We thank Irvin Barouse for being a constant inspiration during Michael's high school years and for always being supportive of his projects, ideas, and dreams.

The faculty, staff, and administration of Archbishop Rummel High School deserve thanks for their patience. A special thanks goes to Denise Otillio for introducing Michael to his passion in writing and to Chuck Guajardo for instilling in Michael his passion for the stage.

The faculty, staff, and administration of Spring Hill College deserve recognition for their support of this project. Specifically, we wish to recognize Kim Anderson; Noreen Carrocci, Ph.D.; Karen Edwards; Fr. Greg Lucey, S.J.; Mark Priede; and Fr. Steve Sauer, S.J., for their encouragement and "cheerleading" through the entire process of writing this book. They are what make Spring Hill College such a special place.

Michael is also grateful to John Burke for his assistance in allowing him to attend Spring Hill College.

And finally, we owe special thanks to our friends and family:

Thanks to Neil Hatchard, Michael's roommate—for being a great friend and an awesome secretary!

We are eternally grateful for Gail Richardson for her love and support over the years. She is the epitome of what a "teacher" should be.

Special thanks to Michael's family for their unrelenting love and support: Robby, Donny, Danny, and Melanie—they are four of the most incredible people alive—and Michael's grandparents, Nathalie Andree, Pat McMyne, and Bill and Beverly Richmond, whose constant encouragement fills his heart.

For her hard work, creativity, and unfailing friendship, special thanks for this project goes to Jo Hart Long. You are a best friend, FRIEND!

Fabulous friends and family like Aunt Katy, Cheryl Amare, Angie Brewster-Battles, Charlotte Brammer, Kim Campbell, Shirl Chumley, Connie Kinsman, Katheryn Overstreet, Kathleen Pisula, Pat Scanland, Jackie Stewart, and Joy Tucker have helped make Nicole the happy person she is. Thanks for your support and laughter!

Indispensable people in Michael's life such as Nicole Acevedo, Blaine Benge, the Benge family, the Dublikar family, Stephen Mount, and the Mount family, who remind him what friendship really is. Additionally, Michael wishes to recognize the members of Mobile Hall's "3W" and all of his other friends at Spring Hill. DELAWARE WHAT?

Very special thanks to Mike Reed and Gordon Stevens for inspiring Michael in more ways than they will ever know.

Special thanks to each and every one of Nicole's students over the past decade.

These acknowledgments would not be complete without thanking Doug, Nicole's husband, for his love and loyalty, without which this project would not have been possible.

MICHAEL McMYNE

SIGNIFICANT CHANGES have occurred culturally that exacerbate the differences between the college students of today and those of even ten years ago. If you dare to venture back in time to the 1980s and even further, the 1970s, the ideology you will uncover will seem antiquated at best and prehistoric at worst. Reaching and teaching students is what many in the Boomer, Mature, or X generations strive to do, but is it feasible for a dinosaur to teach a computer whiz how to live, learn, and flourish?

Just as often as Halley's Comet zooms past our planet are we blessed to have the opportunity to glimpse the ethereal glow of a bright light of knowledge and wisdom, and it is even better when this light emanates from one whose generation we seek to teach. Research has long shown that peer educators are more effective in teaching their own generation than people of another generation are. Such is the case we have here, and such is the information we have within *Real Life University*.

Michael McMyne has faced a lot more adversity in his life than most people. Real adversity. Not "oh no, I wanted a SUV and my parents bought me a station wagon" or "I have to work to pay my way through college because my parents want me to learn self reliance," but actual life-threatening, and in his case, life-affirming, adversity. The *only* way you will know this, though, is if he tells you. All outward appearances suggest Michael has had a normal, albeit rather easy, life. To the contrary, he has not; yet he remains positive, uplifting, caring, and concerned with others. John Donne once wrote, "Any man's death diminishes me because I am involved in mankind." Michael is indeed one of the few—particularly of college students—who is certainly involved in mankind.

In *Real Life University*, Michael has agreed to share the skills he has learned so that other people of his generation would not have to bear the burden of graduating from the school of extremely hard knocks. Reading through the chapters of this book, I found myself chuckling aloud as I recalled struggling with some of the items that seem mundane now but when first attempted seemed impossible. *Real Life University* gives one the hope needed to survive and the sense of humor one needs to flourish. The underlying theme to the book is to "Take a risk." Without risk, one can never hope to succeed because failing, on occasion, is what makes us learn which path is the correct path to take. Edison once said, "I never failed when trying to make the electric light; I first learned about ten thousand things which do *not* make the light work." I implore you to read these chapters and take a risk. You might be surprised at the light that goes on.

Gary Conner

NICOLE AMARE

THOSE WHO EXPERIENCE the "college life" take away with them different memories; most remember dorm life, parties, friends, etc. Very few will admit to carrying with them the memory of a teacher. Nicole Amare is one such teacher who made an important enough impression on me throughout the second semester of my freshman year that to this day I still openly discuss the positive interaction I had with her. As a reader and a student of *Real Life University*, you too will discover in this book what it means to have a teacher who is self-less enough to explain in detail what you can do to succeed.

Ms. Amare was my instructor for English 102, a required class that I assumed would not capture my interest. Glad to be proven wrong, I soon learned what it was like to work with Ms. Amare. It was simple for me to pick up on her natural talents. Her inviting personality and natural high inspired those students who were typically indifferent to learning and reaffirmed those students who were already intrigued by what gifts a wealth of knowledge can bring. She redirected those students who didn't mind school (but needed a slight push) while simultaneously encouraging students who simply couldn't care less about what went on in class. It is said that a student mind learns best if it is opened by a caring and pas-sionate teacher. Nicole Amare is the epitome of that which implements healthy, productive, and progressive learning. *Real Life University* is a product of her passion, which was constructed to help as many students as possible.

Even though I had been a university student for an entire semester (and made it!), I still felt a bit shaky about the whole "college" thing. By the second semester, I was not completely confident about myself either inside or outside of the classroom. However, the classroom environment that Ms. Amare created was one of comfort and ease. She demonstrated herself as more than a teacher to us, which made us more willing to open ourselves up to her and to the other students. Ms. Amare called on us to have an intimate connection with her class while maintaining the already present "teacher/student" bond. She broke stereotypes for us with anecdotes, which provided us thick-headed freshman with a bit of wisdom.

Aside from the knowledge I gained on typical English 102 subjects—reading, writing, and thinking critically—I learned important "real-life" skills that helped me to excel in the class and that are still applicable to me today. For example, Ms. Amare began enthusiastic discussions, but then allowed us students to carry the conversation for ourselves. We developed practical conversation and listening skills under her direction. With this approach, she has made us capable of handling healthy debates and worthwhile exchanges. These valuable discussions and irreplaceable bits of her college expertise permeate the pages of *Real Life University*.

Because Nicole Amare is special by nature and because she is not afraid to share her faults, weaknesses, and mistakes with her students and her readers, we as learners can (either consciously or subconsciously) begin to recognize virtues and vices in ourselves, making it easier for us to mature at a quicker rate. We can more clearly see the reality of situations and adjust our thoughts to make better, more rational decisions. Most importantly, we learn to acknowledge those teachers who make extra efforts to recall the college student mentality in order to help make the transition for us students smoother. Ms. Amare's compassion is evident through example, actively displaying how to think of ourselves more positively and confidently so that we can better empathize with others, especially those who are most different from us.

As you read what Nicole Amare volunteers to enlighten you about, you as a student and an individual will become smarter, more objective, and more confident. I congratulate you on taking the first step toward coming to understand and intelligently deal with your independence by reading this text. The direction and insight provided within the pages of this book will give any reader the same pleasure of learning from Ms. Amare as her students have had.

Mary Whittington

COURSE POLICY

Real Life University

College Student: Michael McMyne
College Professor: Nicole Amare
Where/When: RLU, every day
Phone/E-mail: 1-866-4RLU-RLU;
RLU@reallifeuniversity.com

Required texts: Amare, Nicole, and McMyne, Michael. *Real Life University*. Nashville: Premium Press America, 2002. 160 pp.

Course description: The main purpose of this course is to help students become more successful in college. We will read chapters in *Real Life University* and perform the study exercises in and at the end of each chapter. You will have daily quizzes on real life and four major exams (freshman, sophomore, junior, and senior years). Your final exam will be given the day you graduate and will determine your future success.

Grade breakdown: There are an infinite number of points in this class, so it should be fairly easy to calculate your grade. Students must score 70% or better in order to pass RLU.

90-100%: **A**   80-89%: **B**   70-79%: **C**   Below 70%: **F**

Pop Quizzes	Daily
Yearly (four) Exams	Pass/Fail
Homework	Daily
Attendance/Class Participation	Daily
Final Exam	Pass/Fail
Total	Up to you!

Attendance: Required. If a student misses out on too much of RLU or real life, his or her future may suffer. However, if a student attends every day and is on time for every RLU day, bonus points will be awarded.

Class work and participation: Students will be graded on assigned chapter work as well as class work and participation. Late homework and late class work will not be accepted. Excellent communication skills and willingness to form meaningful and worthwhile relationships will be noted. Students should also participate in at least five activities outside of this class. RLU is a very big campus; please take full advantage of it.

Questions or feedback: If you have any questions or feedback about this course policy, please do not hesitate to contact the student or professor at the contact information listed at the beginning of this course policy.

SYLLABUS

Real Life University

Assignment #1: Read *Real Life University* for the next class; be ready to talk about the most important aspects of the text during class discussion.

FOREWORD

Real Life University

COLLEGE IS A BUSINESS. Sure, universities all across America would like you to view them as a home away from home, a safe haven where you will naturally succeed and prosper, a harbor in the storm of your life. Although universities can be all these things (and much more), you must first of all realize that the college of your choice, like any other corporation, is trying to make money. Your tuition pays for teachers' salaries, new buildings, and the flowers used to decorate the campus lawn. Even if you're a privileged scholarship recipient, your college still wants something from you: brains, sports recognition, musical talent, etc. Good students make good colleges.

Feel like you're going to be used? Don't. After all, you're not the only worker in the college business: the government, private companies, and even former university students (alumni) give money hand over fist to support colleges. Why? Because good colleges also make good students, and these students go on to make successful businesses, schools, companies, cities, and states. The more successful you are in college, the more likely you are to be successful in life.

But what does it mean to be successful in college? Most of us equate school success with grades, but to make it—and we mean really make it—you have to take advantage of your college. That's right: **Use your university**. You pay cash to go to the movies and you expect to be entertained; you shell out money to go out to eat, and you anticipate good service and food; you pay for college, and all you assume you'll get at the end of four or five years is . . . a high-schoolish diploma? While we're pretty convinced that your college of choice will be able to afford that thick piece of scrolled-up paper your degree will be printed on, we're also pretty sure that your thousands of dollars in tuition should, and will, buy you a lot more . . . if you just knew what you could take from your school.

Let's face it: prior to our freshman year in college, most of us have no clue what college is going to be all about. Sure, we know there will be classes and some sports and lots of "meeting new friends and partying!" because our college brother or sister or friend told us these things. But whatever your reason for going to college—to satisfy a scholarship, train for a profession, avoid getting a "real job," do what your parents want/expect you to do, you can't think of any reason not to—wouldn't it be helpful to know what college is *really* about? Wouldn't it be great to know, from an insider's point of view, what actually happens in college: in the classroom, in the dorms, in the professors' offices? Furthermore, wouldn't it be great if you knew how to take full advantage of your years at college?

That's where we come in. Our goal in writing this book is to help future university students like yourself see what college life is really like so that you will have the tools not only to survive, but to excel. As a college student and a college professor, we want to take the secrecy out of universities so that you, the reader, will have the knowledge to be successful in college and in life. Learn from our successes . . . and our mistakes. Figure out how to communicate effectively with other students and faculty members so that you can get the most out of your college years. Build the right relationships to help you earn an A, a scholarship, and even a great job.

If you want to explore the real world of university life—the world where things are not necessarily taught only within the walls of the classroom—just turn the page.

Welcome to Real Life University.

INTRODUCTION

Real Life University

FALL SEMESTER:
From the Student . . .

Michael's Message

A S I WALKED out onto the stage of my first professional speaking engagement, I took a sideways glance at the audience. More than eight hundred pairs of eyes from the auditorium audience—some bored, some angry, some sleepy—were upon me.

"How long have you been a speaker, Michael?" quipped the announcer.

"Since the day my parents' doctor turned me upside down and whacked my bottom," I shot back.

The audience broke out in laughter. I took a determined step toward the front row of crinkled eyes.

"Who *are* you?" My target was a giggly frail girl with a low brown ponytail and a RUSH RULES! T-shirt.

She couldn't have been more than 14; her lithe freshman frame shook rapidly with each gasp and laugh.

I aimed again. "Do you know?"

Her laughter stopped suddenly. She stared at me blankly, then fearfully as the seven hundred ninety-nine pairs of eyes that once threatened to devour me were now peering toward the front row where the girl sat.

"I'm—I'm not sure what you mean," stuttered the now burgundy-faced girl, grabbing at the tips of her hair with her thumb and forefinger. "I dunno."

I shot a toothless smile at the girl, who by now had slumped so far down into the seat that I could barely see her. She looked like a baby kangaroo that was attempting to hide inside her mother's pouch, the folded auditorium seat.

"I didn't know either," I murmured in a low whisper, but still loud enough for the rest of the students to hear. "But I wish I could have figured 'me' out sooner than I did."

I then proceeded to tell my story to those brown eyes, and to all the other eyes in the theater. I began with the verbal and physical mistreatment I had endured for most of my life from two of my brothers, then moved cautiously into the episode where my brother's attempted suicide had almost splintered our family's already-fractured house of glass. I chronicled my twin brothers' gang days, the healing powers of the two women who plucked them from the jaws of death, and my own struggle with physical and emotional mortality at the hands of COPD (Chronic Obstructive Pulmonary Disorder). I walked the group of students through the physical pain of having a laryngoscope coiled in my sinus cavity for 10½ hours, the emotional disappointment of discovering I had been diagnosed with ADHD (Attention Deficit Hyperactive Disorder) and dyslexia (all on top of COPD), and the spiritual grief at the realization that I would always be two steps behind everyone else. When I had reached the valley of my story, I again turned to Miss Low Ponytail in the front row:

"What do you want out of your life? What do you want when you go to college?"

The girl did not speak, but her eyes told me exactly what she did want from me: to leave her alone and to please go and pick on someone else!

I decided to let her off the hook. "It took me fifteen years to find myself," I lunged at whoever in the audience would grab. "How long do you want to wait?"

As soon as I had finished, the eight hundred pairs of eyes lifted themselves three feet higher; the students were giving me a standing ovation for my first public speaking engagement. Now it was my turn to slump and blush. I took a bow, ran behind the stage, and wept with joy. It was at that point in my life that I realized that many students—both high school and college—struggle with trying to find out "who they are." After that presentation, the same brown-eyed girl whom I questioned during my talk came up to me and told me how much my presentation affected her. She continued by telling me that it was not just what I said, but it was because I was only four years older than she that she could relate to what I was saying.

That response has seemed to be the common denominator in my speaking career for the past three years. The majority of the feedback I get from students all across the country is that they feel, live, and experience the same things I feel, live, and experience, which allows them to connect with me and to trust that what I am telling them is what "really happens." The idea for this book came out of that need to reach people outside of the high school and college students I talk to during my presentation.

Oftentimes people say college is a time to figure out who you are, and to an extent they are right. But what they don't tell you is that you don't have four years to figure everything out. The majority of students who enter their freshman year come into college with the high school mentality of life, the mentality that being liked, popular, and accepted are the key elements to their success. However, that mentality needs to end the day of high school graduation, if not sooner.

SPRING SEMESTER:
From the Professor . . .
Nicole Looks Back

I MET Michael McMyne during my first semester of adjunct teaching at a small private college. I wish my initial impression of Michael were a positive one. This beginning day of English 102 consisted of the normal teaching routine I had come to expect over the past nine years: Students listened as I went over the course require- ments, nodded at my questions, and predictably laughed at my horrible jokes. Michael was in the second English class of the morning; he sat front and center, legs crossed widely, his right ankle shaking uncontrollably atop a bare and skinned left kneecap. As he leaned back in the small, wooden desk, I immediately sensed an air of cockiness, of defiance, and of control. I had entered the class expecting the students to hush on this first school day, as they nor- mally do, but Michael kept chatting away to three boys to his left, all the while twirling his pencil, shaking his ankle, and biting his left forefinger at the same time. *Why is he so fidgety?* I immediately thought to myself. *Why doesn't he lower his voice or shut up so I can get started?*

It was day number one, class number one at a new

school in a new city, and I was already thinking to myself: "Great. Here's my 'problem student' for the year." Bah, humbug. Every year at least one student gives me an extremely hard time and disrupts the classroom dynamic. Although I consider myself lucky—one problem student out of approximately two hundred a year is not bad—I, like many teachers, resent the power that one student can have over an entire classroom. For example, a student's loud conversation (especially if it is one chronicling the events of the previous weekend, no holds barred), laughter, or even body language can convince the other students that this teacher and this class are not to be taken seriously. You know the type—the class clown, the sarcastic joker, the flirt, etc.

Almost every teacher has a type of student that s/he dreads having in class. What are these student types? Based on conversations with hundreds of teachers over the past decade, I have created this list of some characteristics of these students who, for one reason or another, want to disrupt the teacher, the class, and everyone else. Although many of these students are not necessarily aware that they are making trouble, this list will help you notice some potential behaviors in yourself that you probably don't want to emphasize in the classroom. If you master the smiles instead of the frowns, you will avoid the dreaded POPS in your college career.

Some **P**itfalls **O**f **P**roblem **S**tudents (POPS)

☹ *The Objector:* Student who brings his or her favorite "object" to class (cell phone, pager, palm pilot, date book, skateboard, nail file, etc.) to class and proceeds to pay more attention to this object than to the instructor or class discussion. Some students also get labeled as problem students by reading newspapers and magazines during class or, more commonly, doing homework in class. Many teachers write this student type off as having a bad attitude.

☺ Instead of being an objector, be a *subjector*—that is, some who is genuinely interested in the *subject* matter of the class. It doesn't matter if it's calculus and you hate math, or Shakespeare's *King Lear* and you hate literature; be as interested and respectful as possible. When you pretend to pay close attention to someone (go on—act a little if you have to!), you may actually find yourself listening and learning a lot.

☹ *The Sleeper:* Student who sleeps in class, stares out the window, or gazes into his/her own "twilight zone." He's the cousin of the objector, but he has no toys to play with.

Real Life University: Orientation

☺ This one's easy: Wake up. Drink coffee, soda, or whatever it takes; a sleepy student is never a successful student. What would class be like if your teacher spent half the time staring out the window? Your credibility as a student is wrecked if your professor catches you dozing off even one time.

☹ *The Sensitizer:* Student who is overly sensitive (whiner, can't take criticism, asks for special treatment: grade changes, extensions on assignments, etc.) Oftentimes this student has no sense of humor and assumes the teacher is always out to "get" him or her. This student thinks everything should be given to him or her, when in fact it is the student who should be trying to earn respect, getting good grades, etc. One typical line often heard from the Sensitizer (asking the teacher): "Are you mad at me?"

☺ Get a backbone. Develop skin thick enough to take constructive criticism. One of the purposes of going to college is to help you grow and improve as a person— and that means some criticism and change. One reason universities call a lot of the classes you take *Humanities* courses is because, among other things, you are learning how to be a better *human* being.

☹ *The Interrupter:* Student who constantly interrupts the teacher and other students. The Interrupters love to pop up with "Can't we take the test next week?" or "Are we getting out early today?"

☺ Another easy one: Just shut up when the teacher or another student is talking, listen respectfully, and raise your hand or make eye contact with the teacher before you are ready to respond. College professors love a student who discusses topics well, asks questions, and participates, but what we don't like is a maniacal egomaniac who hogs the floor and never lets anyone get a word in edgewise. Remember, the smartest people in this world say a few choice words sporadically and strategically, and they don't feel as if they need to prove how smart they are to everyone else.

Men of few words are the best men. —Henry V, William Shakespeare

---

MOST TEACHERS—about ninety-five percent— are not out to get you; they're just doing their job when they grade you strictly and criticize your papers, exams, and projects. Don't take it personally: They are commenting on your work, not judging your worth as a human being. If college were warm and fuzzy, it wouldn't be called college—it would be called day care.

That being said, in your university years you may encounter one or two professors who are out to get you, although you can minimize this occurrence by avoiding POPS-like behavior. Dr. Joe Jerk may refuse to answer your questions, avoid meeting you during office hours, or be excessively unreasonable in his grading. If you come across a bona fide jerk or two, you can always go to a dean at your school for help. (See Chapter 4: Focusing on the Future.) Fortunately, most deans at colleges see students as "customers" whose needs, up to a point, should be met so that the customer doesn't take his or her tuition money elsewhere.

In the meantime, if you're having a problem in a class, your best option is to *ask* for help. Most professors I know are more than willing to help out a student who is eager to learn how to do better (see Chapter 2: Counting on Communication), not those who just come into to our offices to complain about a grade. Outside of teacher assistance, most campuses have tutors, writing and computer labs, and even online labs to help students. The resources are *always* there—your job is to have the courage to ask for help. No one ever makes it to the top without a leg up!

Okay, I know what you're think-

If you come across a bona fide jerk or two, you can always go to a dean at your school for help.

ing, "Wow, this teacher is high maintenance! I hope I don't get someone as demanding as her!" Michael and I did not hit it off those first few classes. But, you already know that Michael could not have turned out to be that much of a problem student, or we wouldn't have written this book together. What you don't know is that teachers, no matter how nice or fair or easy-going, really do resent some of their students all of the time, or all of the students some of the time. Professors are like parents: We generally care for you very much and want you to do well, but at the same time we are human and can be persuaded *not* to like you if you push us far enough. Moreover, certain professors start off the semester by disliking all of their students (or at least they pretend to: I remember one professor during my junior year of college who told us that, as far as he was concerned, "As of the first day of class, all students in this class are failing," and it was up to us to "prove to the professor" that we were worthy of a passing grade) and never really like you until you do something extraordinary. And no, a professor doesn't have to like you in order for you to do well in a class, but wouldn't it be nice to be recognized as the student who shines for your exceptional work ethics

No one ever makes it to the top without a leg up!

and attitude rather than the one who stands out as a troublemaker?

So, other than steering clear of the POPS, how can you make sure you project yourself in a positive way to your peers and teachers during your college years? One method, as Michael mentioned, is to try to figure out "who you are" early enough to allow it to make a difference. Students who know what they want from colleges and where they are going with their lives are the most successful during and after college. Why? It is because these students are aware of their professional and personal needs and desires, and they aren't afraid to "use their universities" to the fullest extent.

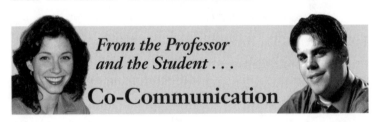

From the Professor and the Student . . .

Co-Communication

Unfortunately, undergraduates with POPS don't have any kind of self-concept or consideration for others. POPS behavior demonstrates a lack of drive, respect, and self-knowledge. Once you gain some confidence and the ability to assess yourself and others accurately, however,

you will begin to recognize the most important requirement of college success:

RLU Requirement #1 YOU—not your par-

ents, teachers, coaches, friends, siblings, or classmates—are the only person who can decide whether
or not you will succeed during and after college.

We have written this book not only to show you the
real world of college life from the perspective of a college professor and a student, but also to provide you with
some valuable tips on how to reach your fullest potential
as a student and as a human being.

You're probably thinking at this point, "Do I really
need a book that tells us how to make it in college?" One
reason you might is because there are so many *unsuccessful* students in college. According to the ACT (American
College Testing program), the college student dropout
rate between freshman and sophomore year is about
twenty-five percent for both private and public institu-
tions, whereas the college graduation rate is roughly
fifty percent.[1] That means that you have a pretty good
chance—approximately seventy-five percent—of making

---

[1] "College Dropout Rate Improves, But Graduation Rate Falls." ACT Newsroom (February 16, 2000)
http://www.act.org/news/innews/index.html 05 October 2001.

it to your sophomore year in college, but you have a much *lower chance of graduating*—about one in two. So, if you're sitting in either your high school classes or one of your freshman college lectures, look around you: Nearly three-quarters of your classmates will be with you next year, but only about one-half of those will be with you when you walk down the stage to receive your university diploma.

Students drop out of college for a number of reasons, and to be brutally honest, being a college dropout does not necessarily mean you'll be a failure in other areas of your life. (See Chapter 2: Counting on Communication.) But if you are already in college or have plans to attend in the near future, then you are already aware of the immense costs to get a college degree these days. Lack of funds or anxiety over growing loan debt is one of the major reasons why students leave school. Rises in tuition costs alone in the past two decades have made college unaffordable for most; parental support and/or weekend jobs are not enough, and students are finding that they themselves have to take out hefty student loans *and* work a part-time job just to cover the basics. Sadly, most employment that students get during their college years is not

The dropout rate between freshman and sophomore year is about twenty-five percent.

directly related to their field of study, and many hours that could have been spent doing an internship, studying abroad, volunteering for campus or community organizations, or working at a good job are instead spent flipping burgers, waiting tables, or answering phones.

You decide your future. Period.

Don't misinterpret our discussion of preferable employment—sometimes a part-time job in a fast-food joint or a grocery store is the best thing for college students because it helps them realize what they *don't* want to be doing for the rest of their lives. So, other than lack of funds, why else do college students leave universities across America? Most freshman are "inadequately prepared" for college, says Wes Habley, Director of the ACT Office for the Enhancement of Educational Practices. Forty years ago, the average college student completed his or her degree in four years. However, it currently takes students *six to seven* years to finish. Working students make up for a big portion of students taking longer to graduate, but unprepared students—students who switch majors a number of times or are academically unprepared[2] for the rigor of a college

[2] Quattrociocchi, Susan M., Ph.D. "Calling All Parents: Are Your Kids Going to College?" http://www.calltoparents.org/calling.htm October 2001.

schedule—help to prolong (or eliminate!) the graduation process. In an effort to "find themselves" and/or catch up in classes, college students are slowing or, even worse, being left behind.

How do you avoid becoming another college drop-out statistic? A good start is to copy the REQUIREMENT #1 from page 18 about college success and paste it to your mirror or put it in your backpack. You decide your future. Period. No one else can do college for you, and no one but you can make the decision to be happy and successful. All the soul-searching techniques and hard work have to be performed by you and no one else. The main reason many college students aren't as successful as they'd like to be is because of passivity. These students may make it through college and receive that expensive piece of paper at the end of their four, five, six, or seven years, but they reach the end of their college career and ask: "Where did all the time go?" and "What do I do with my life from this point on?" If the student has good enough grades, sometimes s/he may decide on graduate school because school is a "safe" place to hide out when you want to avoid the real world.

Those students who let life's events and other people make their decisions for themselves are often stuck in what we like to call *High School Haven*.

These students may have done well in high school—received good grades, attended some social and athletics events, and felt socially accepted by their peers. But college, regardless of what your high school teachers, parents, or anyone else may have told you, is not an extension of high school—or at least, it doesn't need to be. In fact, if your high school experience is anything like both of ours were, you'll be glad to leave high school for a brand new start: college! Because high school success is often based on conformity—what kinds of grades you get, how well you stay out of trouble, and how popular you are—many high school "stars," along with those of us who definitely did *not* have star-like qualities, bomb in college because they fail to make the transition to college life.

Getting out of the *High School Haven* mentality is simple: All you have to do is be NICE.

Network with a wide range of individuals. (Chapter 3)

Investigate yourself first. (Chapter 1)

Communicate effectively with everyone you meet. (Chapter 2)

Expose yourself to extracurricular activities. (Appendix)

The above methods—the core message of this book—are not only great résumé builders, but more importantly, they are the tools required for personal fulfillment, happiness, and success in college and beyond. If you're going to pay thousands of dollars to receive a college degree, you might as well get *all* of your money's worth, right down to the last nickel.

Going to the university of your choice is a lot like going on a job interview.

If you could boil the next few years of your college life into a simple analogy, it would have to be that going to the university of your choice is a lot like going on a job interview because you must:

1. Prepare for the interview by first researching the company.
2. Have a clean, appropriate appearance.
3. Arrive on time and be ready to do your best work.
4. Listen attentively to those around you.
5. Discuss your strengths.
6. Be willing to take constructive criticism and possible rejection.
7. Put your best foot forward.

College is not an extension of high school.

Although attending college four or five years might not be as intense as a two-hour job interview, you will definitely be much more successful in college (and after!) if you approach every class, every professor, and every opportunity with as much enthusiasm and preparation as you would a formal job interview. If you're at your best every day during your college years, you're going to be treated like the best during—when else?—the rest of your "real life" after college.

Clearly we are not saying that you have to don a business suit every day you go to class, but there is something to be said for following the above seven strategies each and every day, and appearance is definitely importance. For example, Nicole had a student a few years ago who wore pajamas and pink fuzzy slippers to every single class. We don't know if this student had lost a bet with her sorority sisters, or if she just felt comfortable wearing her sleepwear to class. She was an excellent writer and a very bright young woman, but it would be difficult to recommend her for a job. It was fortunate that this student never asked me for a letter of recommendation because it would have been hard to avoid discussing her less-than-professional attire in the classroom. What if she wore those clothes all the time, even to a job interview?

We are not saying that you can't be comfortable, but you have to be cognizant of even the smallest things, such as your attire, in class. If you pay attention to these little things, then you are destined to be more successful in and out of the classroom. And you never know whom you're going to have to ask for a letter of recommendation.

Just as the more you prepare for a job interview the better chance you have of getting the job, the more you prepare for college ahead of time the better chance you have of succeeding in and getting the most out of your college years. So, what do you need to do to prepare for the most prospective years of your life? It's simple—just read on, and follow the four steps to college success and happiness!

CHAPTER 1

STARTING FRESH

GET TO KNOW YOURSELF BY YEAR ONE

Real Life University

W**HO *ARE* YOU? Can you write down three of your life goals? Do you know yourself?**

1. Really well!

2. Fairly well

3. Somewhat

4. Um, not really

5. Huh?

Hmm . . . getting to "know yourself" . . . sounds kind of touchy-feely, right? Well, never mind the terminology: the first and single-most important thing you can do for yourself right now, before you go on the big college caper, is to try to figure out who in the heck you are and what you want from your life. Okay, it sounds easy, but sometimes there are a few blinders along the way.

FALL SEMESTER:
From the Student . . .
Michael's Mantra

I HOPE "BECOMING YOU" will be much easier than "becoming me" was, but I wouldn't count on it. It seems that one of the most difficult things we do in college is to transition ourselves from who "we" are at home, as high school seniors, as the sons and daughters of our parents, etc., to who "we" are at college. And, much to my surprise, you begin this transition immediately upon your arrival at college. You might think you've got at least a few practice semesters, but actually every semester counts.

One of the most important things you learn when you arrive at college, or when you chose which college you are going to attend, is that you generally have no idea who you are, what you believe in, and what your goals are. Not to worry, though; you have some time *now* to figure that all out with our help. Uncovering these three ideas are critical to your success, so look seriously at what things *you* believe in, what *your* goals are, and try to separate your own personal agenda from what may be the agenda of other, well-meaning people

In college, every semester counts.

in your life (e.g., parents, teachers, siblings, coaches, etc.). This life is yours and only yours, and since you have to accept the consequences of your actions, you may as well know why you are doing what you are doing.

How do you separate your likes and dislikes from others? Simple: Determine what immediately puts a smile on your face. I can recall the conversation I had with my dad the day that I started my "official college search." We were sitting at the dinner table, and I was trying to get some advice from him as to where I should go to school after high school graduation and what I should study. It seemed impossible for me to think that I was going to have to make this *huge* decision all on my own. I was positive that my parents would help, and ultimately (though I would never admit this during that time) was hopeful that they would decide for me.

My dad just looked at me and said, "Son, I can't help you on this one—you have to make this decision on your own." He went on to tell me that I had to do whatever would make me happy. He told me that the biggest mistake some of his friends made was to go to the college of their parents' choice, and pursue a degree in the same field that their parents were in. My dad then told me there was no way he was going to let me fall into the same boat that his friends fell in. The only suggestion he gave me was to get out a piece of paper and make a list of my likes and dislikes as well as my strong points and weak points. He assured me that this list would help me make this decision. At first, my dad's words and suggestion really angered me—there was no way I wanted to sit and make a list like that because it sounded like the stupidest and most immature idea ever—but I did it, and this activity helped me more than I could ever imagine.

When I reflect on our conversation now, my dad did offer advice . . . the best advice I ever could have received. At the time of our conversation, I was angry because he was not telling me "what I wanted to hear," but rather he was telling me what I *needed* to hear. Now that I have made my decision of where to go to college, I can reflect on that conversation I had with my dad and appreciate what he did for me.

Just as my father once suggested that I start my own list of likes and dislikes to help me make a decision, you may want to create your own **Life-Jacket List** to help you figure out who you are, what you are doing, and where you want to be in

"Son, I can't help you on this one— you have to make the decision on your own."

five weeks, five months, or even five years from now. In the lines below or on a separate sheet of paper, make a list of no less than ten things, no matter how silly or serious, that you like to do in your spare time. Try to list more than ten if you can. Remember, these items are things *you* enjoy, not what your parents/teachers/coaches/ siblings think you should like doing.

If, for example, you like earning and managing your allowance, you may be well on your way to being a CPA. Enjoy sports? Other than being a professional athlete, what about being a recruiter or even writing for a famous sports magazine? At age sixteen, I put down on my **Life-Jacket List** that I love talking to people *all the time*, so, you probably won't find it too surprising that I became, among other things, a public speaker.

RLU Life-Jacket List

1._____
2._____
3._____
4._____
5._____
6._____
7._____
8._____
9._____
10._____
11._____
12._____
13._____
14._____
15._____

Did you write down at least ten things? Even if you put down "Enjoy movies," who knows? You could be the world's best movie reviewer some day. Take everything you like to do to heart and write it down.

The above inventory of what makes you happy in life is called a **Life-Jacket List** because this list may very well "rescue" you some day. Save this list throughout the end of high school and throughout your college career, and pull it out during those times of indecision. After talking with thousands of high school seniors and freshman college students about the most difficult decisions they have faced, I noticed some common trends. Students all across America wonder:

- Where in the world do I want to go to college?
- Do I want a private or public school? Should I attend a small or large school?
- What should be my major?
- What kind of job should I get in college?
- What kinds of clubs and organizations should I belong to in college?
- Should I do an internship or a co-op? What about a junior-year abroad?
- Should I transfer schools?
- What kind of career do I want to pursue after I graduate?
- Do I want to go to graduate school?

Just as my dad mentioned to me about his friends blindly following in the school and career footsteps of their parents, I have several friends in college who are majoring in the same field that one or both of their parents work in, which is great *if* they are doing it because that is what they want to

Enjoy watching movies? Become a movie reviewer.

do. Nevertheless, leaving the values of parents behind is oftentimes an important first step in finding and defining yourself. Watch out for the "parent trap," where you take on one of your parent's professions because the familiar is easiest for you. For example, if you've been surrounded only by psychology books because one of your parents is a counselor, you might want to avoid taking psychology your first semester in college.

> Watch out for the "parent trap," where you take on one of your parent's professions because it's easy.

It is somewhat difficult to succeed in the early years of college unless you have defined who you are—if not to others, then at the very least to yourself—so I recommend taking some time each day to look into your heart (or a mirror) and to ask yourself, "Is this the person who I really am?" or, more importantly, "What do I need to do to make myself the person I want to be five years from now?" The **Life-Jacket List** and a few moments of daily introspection will do wonders for your confidence and will help you set and achieve your goals.

BELOW IS AN INVENTORY of what some incoming freshman in colleges across the nation have said about themselves in response to questions about why they wanted to come to college. Do you see yourself in any of these students? Do you notice any of the "I vs. my parents" mentality surfacing? In your opinion, who has already assessed his or her own personal needs and goals, and who on the list still needs to get a clue?

"I am going to college to become a nurse because my mom's a nurse. It seems like a good job and she likes it." —Jamie Cary, Lansing, Michigan

"Why I am going to college? I dunno—I never thought I *wouldn't* go to college. I mean, doesn't everybody go to college?"—Sam Nguyen, Seattle, Washington

"All I know is that I'm majoring in business so I can make a lot of money." —David Wells, Wichita, Kansas

"To learn the skills that will land me a good job and broaden my perspective on life."—Chico LeBato, Mobile, Alabama

"I think I want to be a lawyer. I'll be a good lawyer, or at least my folks seem to think so—they are always saying I'd make a great lawyer someday because I am so good at arguing with them."—Sarah Kasper, Baton Rouge, Louisiana

"All I know is that I'm going to a college that has a high female-to-male ratio. I want to up my chances of meeting some good-looking girls."—Angelo Ricardo, Buffalo, New York

"I am attending college on full academic scholarship. I am the first person to attend college in my entire family, so like everyone in my family is so proud of me. I have already decided to major in pre-med because I am eventually going to be a pediatrician."—Tamilla Jackson, Atlanta, Georgia

"I picked my college because all my friends were going to [the same school]. I didn't want to go to a school where I wouldn't know *anybody*!"—Chris Dietrich, Harrisburg, Pennsylvania

"My coach is the reason I'm here. I wouldn't have picked [this school] were it not for him."—Jeremy Ulman, San Francisco, California

"As an International Business and Spanish double major, I plan to spend my junior year abroad in Madrid. They say there's no better way to learn a language than to be in the country for a long time. I hope to be a translator for the Pentagon someday." —Emile Gutierrez, El Paso, Texas

"My father wants me to major in business, but I love art. I have tried to talk to him about it, but he says since he pays the tuition, I have to major in what he says. I have six younger siblings counting on me to graduate and get a good job that will make some money, and I don't know many artists who make a decent living. So, I guess I'm a business major with a really great hobby."—Victoria Searing, Parker, Colorado

Okay, now it's your turn to give your quote. In the space provided, fill in you answer to the following questions: What type of college do you want to go to and why? What do you want to major in and why?

You can send your answers to these questions now to RLU@reallifeuniversity.com for a chance to see it in our next book!

SPRING SEMESTER:
From the Professor . . .

Nicole's Knapsack

DON'T PANIC right away if your **Life-Jacket List** surprisingly consists of your doing things that your parents expect you to do. We spend many years being rewarded in school and at home for obedience, and for some of us, it is hard to break out of the "parent-pleaser" mold. It sure was difficult for me. I went to school in my hometown because I was too afraid (or unsure, or apathetic) to move away and "find myself." In college, I gravitated only toward disciplines I excelled in and, although I am ashamed to say it now, I definitely steered away from courses that looked too challenging. What happened to my four years at college, you ask? I wasted them—every last year. I joined no clubs, no organizations, and did not volunteer for any community agencies or internships.

In sum, I am the classic example of what happens when college students don't take the time to self-reflect enough to know how to use their universities to help them succeed in life. I had to spend almost a decade in graduate school to "know myself," and while everything is all right now, I know I lost a lot of valuable time because I was one of those unprepared students. On my college graduation day, I certainly didn't have any feelings of personal accomplishment, and I had no job prospects. My first college graduation job was selling cutlery door to door. I had waited too long to start building a résumé. Fortunately for you, this book shows you how to avoid the obstacles we didn't. Learn from our mistakes.

If your life is anything like mine was in high school, I am sure you have plenty of people breathing down your neck telling you that college is "more than the classroom." Where I hope your college life differs from mine is that you listen to what those people are telling you because they are exactly right. If you fail to get involved in your college, you are drastically decreasing your chances of getting that dream job you are searching for.

Statistics prove that employers are much more inclined to hire a candidate with good grades and extracurricular

> We spend many years being rewarded for obedience, and it is hard to break out of the "parent-pleaser" mold.

activities rather than one who only went to class and did the bare minimum and maybe worked a crummy part-time job. Potential employers want you to have extracurricular activities under your belt before you walk into your job interview. Why? Because employers see students who are involved in campus and community organizations, clubs, and internships as "go-getters" who are used to working with others. People who do well on the job in the "real world" learned collaboration, cooperation, and communication with others in campus organizations. If all you've accomplished after four years is attending class, all your employer thinks you know how to do is be an obedient student. And, being a classroom-only student really doesn't prepare you for real life outside of university walls. Volunteering for an organization or doing an internship, for example, can be a valuable stepping stone to your life after college.

An internship can be a valuable stepping stone toward your career after college.

So, if you don't feel like making the same mistake waiting around to figure out what you want out of life, listen up, because this next section will make the transition easier for you. I have found after talking with thousands of students is that the first thing many high schoolers need before they can "get to know themselves" is to have the opportunity and the time to be left alone. All throughout high school (and college, for that matter), you are constantly surrounded by people everywhere and all the time. How are you supposed to figure out what makes you an individual if you haven't had any time to *be* independent? The few steps below will get you started; some of them may seem tough, but the best way to understand your own personal needs and desires is to separate them from the many people (gazillions!) around you.

Soul-Searching Steps

Keep a journal. Write down day-to-day events, thoughts, or anything that comes to your mind; the important thing is to write something about yourself and your experiences on a regular basis (daily, weekly, or monthly). You can look back on the journal at a later date to figure out how you solved a personal problem or conquered a dilemma. Writing is one of the best forms of self-reflection and discovery around.

Go to a movie—by yourself. What movie did you choose? Did you find that you enjoyed the movie, or did you concentrate more on the surroundings? What did you learn about yourself from this experience?

Eat out—alone. If you can't handle the thought of

an entire meal in a public place without someone at your table to talk to, go ahead and bring a book, magazine, or newspaper. What did you notice about the experience? Did you find that you talked to the server or host or manager more? Did you strike up conversations with other people in the restaurant, or did you bury your head in your meal/book/paper?

Take a walk—without a Walkman. Walk for at least thirty minutes. Take note of any items or thoughts that you dwelled upon that you might not have if you had walked with a friend or a Walkman.

Go for a drive. Or, if you don't have a car, ride your bike, or scooter, or skateboard, or rollerblades. See where your transportation leads you, and remember what you notice and think about on your journey.

Do some shopping—without friends. Check out what stores you go to. If you're not a shopper, sit on a bench in a busy mall and people watch. What do you notice about others that may not have caught your attention before?

Self-assessment is one of the most positive things you can do to make yourself successful; there are also some things you should try to avoid. There are only two things out there in RLU Land wait-

> **Self-assessment is one of the most positive things you can do to make yourself successful.**

ing to ruin your college career and any future chance at happiness: Fear and Apathy. Let's tackle the big "F" word first: *fear*. If you fear change—if you fear breaking the mold your parents have so safely provided for you because you are afraid to do the unfamiliar or the uncomfortable—then there are not as many opportunities for you. Theoretically, you can walk in Mommy's or Daddy's footsteps and take over their jobs when you grow up, and possibly become very wealthy. And it is fine if you choose this path if, and only if, you can truly state from the bottom of your soul that you enjoy doing your parent's work—because if you don't, you will find yourself unsuccessful in a very crucial area of your life: personal fulfillment. Everyone knows that unhappy people make bad bosses, spouses, parents, employees, etc.

More often than not, however, Fear leads to that other dreaded "F" word: *failure*. Fear is the number-one reason we don't learn about or seek out new friendships, internships, jobs, and changes for personal happiness. Fear keeps us from asking our professor a question or our bosses for a raise. Being afraid closes the doors to the successes we all deserve in life, especially during our college years.

To help you get a little grounded into how fear is connected to failure, write down at least five things you are afraid will happen to you in college. It is important to be as honest with yourself as you can. What is it that worries you the most? Once you acknowledge your own fears, you are well on your way to conquering them:

1. _____
2. _____
3. _____
4. _____
5. _____
6. _____
7. _____
8. _____
9. _____
10. _____
11. _____
12. _____

What's the opposite of fear? It's not security—it's Courage. There are some other nice "C" words that go along with courage; let's call them the Three C's.

Three C's:
Challenge   Chance   Change

It's your job, as a college student, to challenge yourself, take chances, and allow yourself some room to change. College is a time to break your old habits and traditions and explore new things. It would be a huge mistake for you to fear change. The students who are most successful during and *after* their college careers are those students who were willing to take a few risks, try some of the hard classes, and talk to professors and advisors about questions or interests they have.

Most importantly, don't let fear of bad grades keep you from success. Some years ago, a mechanical engineering professor told me that he noticed during his twenty years of teaching engineering that the most successful engineers who were once in his class were *not* always his A students, but rather his B and even his C students. Why did this professor view his so-called average or above average students as the winners after college? He noticed that the B and C students graduated and went on to entrepreneurial-type jobs; apparently they weren't happy as entry-level engineers or even middle managers, so they often started their own companies. And the A students? Well, this one professor noticed that theses students, who had been bright and obedient in the

Grades do matter—but they are not the only keys to success.

classroom, continued to be bright and obedient outside the classroom. In fact, the former A students did so well at their current jobs that they often did not feel the need or desire to move up or leave the company. Although the outstanding students usually made very good employees, they often felt secure in their jobs and—yup, you guessed it—they began to fear change, and they didn't challenge themselves. The average students, on the other hand, thought they had nothing to lose, and took many more chances in life, risks that ultimately opened new and successful doors for them.

While I recognize that this professor's assessment of students is very anecdotal and overly generalized, I would not have recounted his observations here if I had not noticed a similar trend in my own classes. For example, about six years ago I had a woman in my English class—let's call her Amanda—who was a horrible student; she rarely came to class, and her writing was very shallow and rushed. She came into my office one day during my office hours early in the semester to talk to me about her poor performance. I was ready for the standard excuses (my boyfriend left me, I've been personally ill, my grandmother/uncle/dog/pet rock died, etc.) for why she was not doing very well in my class. It turned out that this student worked for a local domestic violence shelter for many hours a week, and her schedule was very erratic. I started to give her the speech about the rules of the class when I noticed the title on the blue notebook she was holding: Writing Therapy Sessions. When I inquired about the notebook, the student explained that she had been neglecting her writing assignments in my class because she spent many of her hours teaching the domestic violence victims how to express their thought in journals, or "writing therapy."

This idea of helping battered women recover through writing was so intriguing to me that the student and I worked out a plan where she could include some of her written observations and analysis of the therapy sessions as part of her writing assignments for my class. Although I recognize that not all professors are able to accommodate students in such a manner, I realized from this student that even though she was a C student in my class, she was working outside the classroom to fulfill her dream by doing what she enjoyed. Not only did she not fear getting a bad grade in my class, but her hard work outside the classroom helped to make her personally fulfilled and successful.

Getting involved outside of class may positively influence the work you do in class.

Okay, so what is a college professor doing telling you it's all right to get grades other than A's in college?

While great grades are definitely important if you want to go on to graduate school or receive a scholarship, one of the biggest mistakes I see college students (including myself when I was one) make time and time again is that they are so obsessed about grades and pleasing the professors (or their parents, or both) that they get tunnel vision and miss out on all the opportunities colleges across America have to offer. In short, students who succeed learn how to use their universities. I couldn't agree more with what Michael said earlier about grades: If all you get out of college is a 4.0 and nothing else—no direction about what you want to do with your life, no fulfilling connections with college faculty and other students, no experience in campus organizations, job internships, or junior-year-abroad programs—you may find yourself prepared for only one thing, and that is more school, which is great if you knew beforehand that you planned to attend graduate school. If not, then you need to figure out who you are, what you want, and where you are going.

In many cases, it would probably be better for you to have a 3.0 but a whole résumé full of valuable extra-curricular activities (internships, campus organizations,

> **Students who succeed learn how to use their university.**

volunteer work) rather than a 4.0 with no evidence of being able to accomplish anything outside the classroom. Trust me: Future employers won't be asking you what you did *inside* the classroom (What are they going to ask you about—your note-taking skills? How well you raised your hand to ask a question? Your penmanship?), but what you did with your life *outside* the classroom. I have been to dozens of interviews since college, and even though my interviews have predominantly been at universities, I have never been asked my GPA. It simply does not matter as much. What matters to my future employers is that I prove I am innovative, a good colleague, a cooperative worker, a problem-solver, a leader, and a compassionate individual. I learned all of these skills, as you will, by doing activities other than being a student sitting in college lecture halls.

> **People without passion don't work hard.**

> **Employers won't ask what you did inside the classroom, but what you did outside the classroom.**

Once you have made some decisions about what already brings you some joy and satisfaction in your life, you're ready to conquer the second major obstacle standing in your way: Apathy, or indifference (lack of passion). People without passion don't work hard. How do you avoid apathy? It's not easy. Most of us spend our entire lives fighting the urges to kick back, give up, and be lazy. But once you have an understanding about the goals in your life, your next step is to work intelligently to achieve those goals. Michael's **Life-Jacket List** is a good way for you to get started, but once you make those decisions about the next four years of your life, it's time to determine the best and most efficient ways to reach those goals. People who work hard often achieve their goals, but may find themselves worn out by the time they get there; people who work intelligently achieve their goals and are happy and successful. Let's call these smart workers **Smarties** since they are clever enough to know how to get from point A to B in their lives in the most effective manner possible.

What are some common characteristics of **Smarties?**

SOS—**S**kills **O**f **S**marties

- Always be on time—no matter what the occasion is. If you have something planned, be there early!
- Be happy. Everyone loves a smile and an alert, energetic face.
- Branch out and meet new people. When it's time to join a group, don't join the same group your friends are in.

- Build relation-
  ships with people
  from different
  cultures, religions,
  and backgrounds.
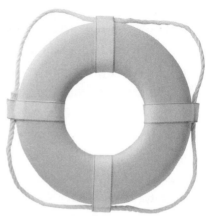
- Finish what you
  start.
- Keep your prom-
  ises. Never give
  others reason to
  not trust you.
- Follow up on appointments, meetings, etc., with
  phone calls and e-mails.
- Know your strengths and weaknesses.
- Learn from your mistakes and your successes.
- Offer help when someone else asks for it. Be
  reliable.
- Rely on other people: you can't do it all, so be
  willing to accept some help.
- Show gratitude: Send thank-you notes.

The best thing about **Smarties** is that they're not an
exclusive club—anyone can be one, especially you!

RLU
Reflection
Section
#1

1. Create a **Life-Jacket List**. Store it someplace safe and where you can retrieve it easily. Feel free to add to it or change items as you grow as a person and as a college student.

2. Write down your three life goals:

   1. _____

   2. _____

   3. _____

What is the number-one most important thing you want to do in your life? _____

_____

What do you want your first job to be after you graduate and why? _____

_____

Where do you see yourself ten years from now?

_____

(Remember, answers to these questions should avoid the "wherever life takes me" angle.)

3. If you are still in high school, make a list of colleges you are considering. Then, write in two separate columns the PROS and CONS for each school. If you can't think of many things to say about the school, you need to do more research: Visit the campus, check the school out on the web, or talk to students or faculty at the school.

COLLEGE CHOICE #1 = _____

PROS	**CONS**
_____	_____
_____	_____
_____	_____
_____	_____
_____	_____
_____	_____
_____	_____

4. If you are already in college and are undecided about a major, do #3 but for your prospective majors. Again, if you don't know enough about the majors, talk to advisors, professors, and students in the individual disciplines. You will also need to talk to a career counselor (every campus should have a career center) to see what kinds of jobs can be gotten with certain majors. Learning what kind of employment you'll be able to get (or not get) sometimes swings your decision drastically in one direction.

My ideal major = _____

Second option for major = _____

Third option for major = _____

Kinds of jobs I can get with my major:

_____

_____

_____

_____

_____

5. What are your three biggest fears in life?

1. _____

2. _____

3. _____

Next, write a plan of action (a strategy) for conquering each fear. How could change or chance help you eliminate your fears?

How I will conquer fear:

1. _____

2. _____

3. _____

6. What are some POPS (see Introduction)? What are some methods you can use to avoid the POPS?

_____

_____

_____

7. Study the SOS section. What are some ways you can apply some or all of these habits to your everyday life?

_____

_____

_____

8. Sit down with one or both of your parents, and ask them what they expect from you in college. Try to get them to be as specific as possible. Then, ask them how they would react if for some reason your college dream didn't end up matching theirs. Show them your **Life-Jacket List** so they have some idea *before you graduate* that your life is not necessarily a mini-version of theirs.

Parent or Guardian #1 expects:

_____

_____

Parent or Guardian #2 expects:

_____

_____

9. Fill in the blanks: "I am _____ today, and I will be _____ someday."

10. After completing some of the **Soul-Searching Steps**, write down how you think you have changed as a person.

_____

_____

_____

_____

_____

_____

_____

_____

_____

_____

_____

_____

_____

CHAPTER 2

COUNTING ON COMMUNICATION

CONTACTS BY YEAR TWO

Real Life University

ARE YOU A good communicator? No matter whether your high school is large or small, public or private, you probably leave home to go to school early in the morning, and then return home every day at 3:00 P.M. (or later, depending on your after-school activities). At college, however, you are on your own—you come and go when you please (for the most part), and you have control over your own hours. Most high school seniors think this freedom is the best aspect of college life, but the problem is that many incoming college freshmen—as well as many existing college students—are not sure how to adapt from high school to the way of life that college offers. What often happens is that once college students get that first taste of freedom, they lose all self-control. This "burden of freedom" ultimately hinders the ability to be successful and get the most out of college life.

In your high school life, you could usually count on your parents and/or teachers to help you communicate or, at least they knew you well enough that they would not criticize your communication mistakes. The biggest adjustment for most college students, other than learning how to be personally responsible for their own lives, is understanding how to communicate effectively with others.

Communication is a tricky term because it *sounds* so easy—pretty much everyone knows how to *physically* talk to others, right? Since you have already gone through the steps from chapter one to figure out what's important to you, now you're ready communicate exactly what you mean to others. Even so, communicating with others—whether it be your roommate, Resident Assistant, professor, dean, or boss—requires you to learn to successfully *connect* to another person or group of people with your *message*. This *message*, of course, can come in a number of forms:

Conducting Connections

- **Tone:** How does my voice sound to other people?
- **Eye Contact:** Do other people see me as trustworthy?
- **Body Language:** What do my body gestures say about me as a person?
- **Volume:** Am I a quiet communicator, or am I too loud?
- **Mouth:** Do I smile a lot, or do I tend to pout? When I am in class or at a meeting, do I sigh a lot?
- **Spoken words:** What does my elevated vocabulary (or slang) say about me? What about my accent?

● **Written Words:** How does what I write in my e-mail messages and class assignments reflect the kind of person I am trying to portray?

Look at the people above. Which one do you want to get to know and why? Although you can't "hear" the volume or tone or the people in the pictures, what do you already know about the people based on their eyes, the shape of their mouth, and body language? What kind of image do you want to portray to your professors and colleagues?

On today's college campuses, the popularity of e-mail is skyrocketing and is taking the place of "snail mail." Oftentimes, your professors will request that you submit course work and handle all outside of the classroom communications with them through the campus e-mail. Additionally, e-mail has made it much easier to keep in contact with your family and friends at home. If you are not careful about what you say in these messages, however, you may find yourself in a big bind. The problem with e-mail is often the way your message reads; you may have no intention to sound rude, aggravated, or disgusted, but your message may portray those characteristics. It is very important that you be careful when you send e-mail messages. Take a look at the following samples of messages that two students sent to Nicole:

E-Mail #1

To: Professor Nicole Amare
From: Sandy Student
Subject: I need help on paper #2

Dear Professor Amare,

My name is Sandy Student, and I am in your MWF EH 101 class at 9:00 A.M. I have a question about paper #2: May we use a personal interview with an expert as a possible source? I know we discussed using library sources in class on Monday, but my topic (campus parking) would benefit from an interview from the Director of Parking Services. Please let me know if I may use an interview as an outside source. Thank you so much for your help. I can be reached at 555-1234, or just hit reply to this e-mail message.

Thanks again,
Sandy

E-Mail #2

> To: Professor Nicole Amare
> From: Anita Gudgrade
> Subject: What's my grade?
>
> hey nicole,
>
> when are we getting our papers back? i'm not tryin to bug you cause i know you jsut gotem yerterday, but I really wanna know my grade ASAP i need an A in this class super bad

What does the language say about the writers? What do you notice about the tone of the message? Which student is more polite, more formal, smarter, and more apt to get a response? Pretend you're the professor and you have over 100 students a semester: which message do you want to receive?

E-Mail Exercise

E-mail example #1 is the kind of e-mail you want to write to your professors: It is polite, clear, and free of errors. Now, practice some effective communication by rewriting e-mail #2, which is a poor example of e-mail communication. Please make sure to revise the tone (make more polite), meaning (make clearer), and typos in the e-mail. Remember: Professors love polite, formal e-mails, especially when it is your first time e-mailing them.

Your revision of e-mail #2 here:

Mirroring the Message Exercise

In order to succeed in college, you will need to work on both written and oral communication strategies. Many of us have heard our voices reproduced on a tape recorder or answering machine. How did you respond the first time you heard your own voice? Were you disappointed? Proud? Embarrassed? Most of us are amazed at how we sound—not like we intended to. So, if your voice sounds so very different on an answering machine, imagine how different you must look when you see yourself on video. While you're at school, at work, or just out and about, have a friend, sibling, or parent videotape you for thirty minutes. This exercise will work best if you don't know you're being videotaped.

1. Does the image of yourself reveal the image that you thought you were presenting?
2. How well do you use your body language? Does your body language communicate the same message your words did?
3. Did you notice any specific problems with your method of communicating? Are there any annoying habits that you were not aware of?
4. Look at all the other people listening to you in the video. How do these individuals respond to you at different times? Try to note what behavior causes the other people to react to you in positive or negative ways. How can you adjust your behavior?

Don't have access to video equipment? Try having a close friend observe your non-verbal communication from a distance. What does s/he notice about your body language?

If you take advantage of the video exercise, however, you will be amazed at the methods in your communication skills that you want to change. Videotaping speakers is a self-improvement method that is used in multiple disciplines and professions. Seeing yourself as others see you is an excellent way for you to "secretly" improve your communication skills.

SPRING SEMESTER:
From the Professor . . .

Nicole's Nitpickins

IF IT WERE POSSIBLE, I wish I had a videotape of every college student in the classroom. As a teacher, I have been videotaped a number of times for evaluation purposes, and I always notice something in my voice or behavior that I try to alter in order to make myself a more effective teacher. If only students could witness their own body language and hear their own voices in the college classroom, they would be shocked. In fact, other students in the classroom often are surprised at the attitudes of their fellow students, but the bad behavior often goes unchecked because the person rarely notices how offended everyone else is because s/he is unable to see his or her own communication mishaps.

Some Pitfalls of Problem Students (POPS) were mentioned in the Introduction, but the list below is a more comprehensive one of observed student behavior, and it is based on interviews with hundreds of professors across the country. You may think these professors have a lot of Don'ts on this list, but this behavior wouldn't be suitable in a business setting either. Your best bet is to start practicing now in college for your real life after college.

Professor's Pet Peeves

Since you're no longer in high school, you can quit acting like you are still getting ready for senior skip day. Follow these Do's and Don'ts to be a successful student inside the classroom:

Do's

- Come to class every day and on time.

- Bring the textbooks, paper, and a writing instrument to every class.

- Get to know a classmate or two or three so you'll have some study partners.

- Meet all deadlines.

- Use the bathroom before coming to class.

- Eat some food before class so you won't be hungry or fatigued during class.

- Maintain eye contact with your professor.

- Take notes! Let me say that one again: TAKE NOTES!

- Participate: Answer questions the professor asks, get involved in a class debate, etc.

- Smile when your professor makes a joke; nod your head occasionally during the lecture to show the professor you are awake and you understand the material.

- Volunteer when the professor asks for help from a student.

- Visit your professor occasionally during office hours so s/he can get to know you. Or, send an e-mail.

- Say please or thank you when your professor does something for you.

- If you need to make up work, ask for a time that is convenient for your professor.

Don'ts

- Disrupt the class by walking in late or leaving early.

- Talk to other classmates, even if it's about class material, while the professor or other students are talking.

- Ask your professor to recap a lecture you missed.

- Ask for special treatment or extensions on your out-of-class work.

- Put your head on the desk.

- Work on other classes (homework, studying for tests, etc.)

- Ask to speak to the professor one-on-one once the class starts. (Wait until after class or during office hours or conferences.)

- Interrupt the professor or other students.

- Monopolize the professor's time when other students are clearly waiting.

- Leave your cell phone or pager on (and please don't answer the phone or pager if you do forget to turn it off! Leave phone and pagers in your car or dorm.)

- Ask when the papers/exams/assignments are going to be passed back.

- Ask "Are we doing anything important today?" or "Can we get out early?"

- Have an attitude: roll eyes, sigh during class, tilt head in disgust, yawn, click pen, etc.

- Pack up early or rustle papers while the teacher or another student is still talking.

- Say "I have to miss the next class because I am getting a haircut/need to pick up my roommate at the airport/have to work/need to study for a test in another class . . . is that okay?"

All of the previous do's and don'ts focus on one special area of communication: respecting others. If you show your professors, colleagues, and eventually your bosses that you have respect for them, there's no telling how far you can go in this world. The sky's the limit!

You need to learn another important area of communication, however: How do you want to communicate outside the classroom? The first thing you learn when you get to college is that you are now living in an environment that you are not yet used to. Don't worry, though; hundreds if not thousands of other people there are also living at a place not yet their home. Take comfort in the fact that you have many compatriots in this venture. Most of these people will not look like, think like, or be like you in an awful lot of ways. College offers diversity in many different forms that for most of us has never been experienced. One of the hardest things to get used to is living with someone else, let alone someone that you don't know. At first, the adjustment seems impossible—you and your roommate have totally different tastes, likes, and dislikes. You are convinced that it is not going to work between two of you: Either you have to go or your roommate has to go. It doesn't matter to you.

Always respect others.

FALL SEMESTER:
From the Student . . .
Mike Meets His Match

T HE FIRST DAY on my college campus I was so
scared. I had no idea what to expect or how to
act. My parents were with me for the move-in process,
which made the transition a little bit easier. As soon as I
got to my dorm room to start to move in, I noticed that
my roommate, Grant, was already there. As a matter of
fact, he had unpacked all of his things, taken the bed and
closet of his choosing, and arranged the room the way he
wanted it. I was not too happy that I was going to have to
sleep in the bed against the wall and use the closet behind
the door, especially since the room was only about the
size of my mom's minivan but with a little more head-
room. We only talked once prior to moving in, and that
was to see who was going to bring what appliances, deco-
rations, etc.

The entire time I moved all twenty boxes up the
stairs (hint: you cannot pack your life away and bring it
to college—there is no room!), Grant's parents and mine
began to get to know each other. I figured it would be
a good idea to talk to Grant and get to know him a bit

since I was going to live with him for the next year. As I was walking up the stairs with my huge stereo, instead of offering to help, he asked me what kind of music I listened to. I was annoyed that Grant was not helping me move all the things that we were both going to use, but I just ignored it and I told him that I mostly like all music except rap, and that my favorite music is country. Grant looked at me and said, "I like nothing but rap and particularly hate country!" At that point, I knew were going to have problems. We continued asking each other questions for about the next hour. I went on to tell him that I stay awake very late and sleep in—he informed me that he goes to sleep early and wakes early. I told him that I could not sleep with the TV on, and he, of course, informed me that he only goes to sleep to the sounds of the television. I learned that while I was messy, he was obsessively clean; while I loved English, he was good in math, etc.

That night I went to sleep wondering how in the world I got paired up with this creature. I could not figure out how this bad arrangement happened; after all, the housing office sent all incoming freshmen a form to fill out about ourselves, with a little note that informed us that the form is what they were going to use to match roommates. I was very careful when filling it out, making sure to make my answers to fit the dream of a "perfect roommate." Certainly that form did not pair me with Grant. The first week of living together was total hell for both of us. Prepared to go to the housing office to switch roommates, I was confident that there was someone more like me.

> "If you cop out and change roommates, you are preventing yourself from growing."

As I was voicing my extreme dissatisfaction to a friend before class one day, my history professor overheard me and said: "Michael, this mismatch is a reason for you to grow, and growth is what college is all about. Having Grant as a roommate will allow you to learn about different cultures, and this experience will help you dramatically in your future. If you cop out and change roommates, you are preventing yourself from growing."

I was not sure at that time what my history professor meant, and I was angry that he had not helped me by telling me what I needed to do to switch into another room, but I agreed to try to work it out.

I went back to my room that afternoon and tried to just talk to Grant and really get to know him. By midterms that same semester, Grant was listening to slow country/western, and I knew every lyric to several hiphop and rap songs. I learned to fall asleep to the tunes of the television and actually saw a few times what the early morning sky looked like. The growth process was amazing to me—I reached horizons that I never imagined I would ever hit.

Communicate with as many people as possible.

Unfortunately, Grant decided to leave my college and continue his education elsewhere. Second semester was not the same for me; there were no three-hour conversations with Grant, which I had begun to really enjoy. Instead, I had to just remember the fun times we had as roommates, and thank God that we gave our friendship a chance. I had effectively communicated with and befriended someone completely different from me, which brings us to the second most important requirement of college success: Communicate with as many people as possible.

> **RLU Requirement #2** Try to relate to people extremely different from you. Communicating effectively with people from different cultures, regions, languages, etc., will bring you personal satisfactions and successful relationships.

I like to relate college to a fishbowl. If you are like

most college students out there, your fishbowl is crowded and many of the fish in it (not just your roommate) are not accustomed to the things that you are, and they will not understand some of your idiosyncrasies; since you will not understand many of theirs either, you will have to begin learning and growing right away. As Nicole said earlier, the first important lesson of college is . . . *communication*. Communication at college is different from communicating at home because of the fishbowl and all the fish in it; they are different from you, and not just because they look different. The collegiate fishbowl is full of a diverse group of fish; for many, going to college is the first time in their lives they will face diversity "up close and personal." For example, you will hear accents you never knew existed; see hairstyles and types of dress very different from your own; encounter ideologies (personal belief systems) that radically oppose yours; etc. Therefore, your communication has to take into account the ways different people think, act, feel, and process information. You already know how others see you; now, try to watch how other people present themselves. How are their messages communicated differently from how you communicate?

CAMPUS CONVERSATION DO'S

1. What you are saying is not necessarily the message received by others, so be aware of all your verbal and non-verbal methods of communication.

2. Notice that people from different cultures relay and process information in different manners; don't judge people just because their communication methods are not the same as yours.

3. Take the time to get to know people who are different from you; then ask polite questions when you have that person one-on-one.

4. Be prepared to answer questions about your culture, and remember, others are just as curious about you as you are about them.

5. Be willing to be a bit uncomfortable when first learning about other cultures. Fearing difference is bad; change and growth are good!

When meeting and interacting with people, it is imperative that you be an excellent communicator. Communication, as you already know, is the sending and receiving of messages, which means you will need to learn to speak clearly and listen well. Few people realize that most of the messages we send are sent silently, so understand that communication is much more than just words. We communicate with one another by our posture, our facial expressions, the inflection of our voice, and by things we do not say. So remember that everything—the message you send to others via the clothes you wear, how you decorate your room and living space, and the bumper stickers you place on your car—are all constantly being critiqued. You must remain cognizant of the fact that twenty-four hours a day, seven days a week, you are who you are, part good and part challenging, for all to see. Remain open to those people who seem like your opposite when you first meet them; oftentimes, the way we communicate (both verbally and non-verbally) is the way the people around us categorize us, which means you may look strange to the opposite person, too!

CAMPUS CONVERSATION DON'TS

1. Proxemics, or where you place yourself when communicating to someone else, is extremely important: some people get offended if you stand too close or too far away; try to be open to their reaction to your proxemics.

2. Don't look away from the person. Failure to maintain eye contact throughout the majority of the conversation shows lack of interest and bad manners.

3. When communicating to someone who is angry, avoid a "level-raising voice contest." You'll lose and in more ways than one.

4. Never say one thing to one person and the opposite to someone else . . . they will both find out and neither will ever trust you again.

5. Avoid trying to "out talk" people . . . be a good listener!

Let me give you an example: My friend Allen is a really good guy. He is fun to be with, has good sense of humor, and is a pretty good student in class. All the guys really like him, and I am sure his family does too. The problem is that he does not seem to make friends with members of the opposite sex very easily. He has had a couple of girlfriends, but their friends are never crazy about Allen, and the other girls who hang out with the people I hang out with have not been very close to Allen either. He has always been nice to them, polite and all, but there seems to be a lack of trust or some other barrier he could not get around. I finally asked Donna, another good friend of mine, if she noticed that Allen was not the kind of guy who had many female friends, and why. She said, "Go to Allen's room and look around. That ought to explain it for you."

By now my curiosity was out of control, so I jetted down to Allen's room to follow Donna's advice and "look around." Allen was not in there at the time, but his room-mate Max was, so I asked him if I could come in for a second. I had been in and out of Allen's room all year; once or twice I had even fallen asleep on his carpet while playing video games, but I guess I had never paid much

> **Twenty-four hours a day, you are who you are, part good and part challenging, for all to see.**

attention to anything but the TV and his fridge. The first thing I saw when I looked around was an entire wall covered with Miss this month and Miss that month; Allen's desk had smaller cut-outs off nude or semi-nude females in all types of poses, many of them in the company of other people. (One picture even showcased a Ferrari containing two naked women who seemed quite fond of each other reclining suggestively on the ad, holding the reins of a Clydesdale and looking longingly at a nearby waterfall.)

I began to understand why women kept a distance from Allen . . . they figured he thought of them as objects and not people, so they did not trust him. I asked Donna if this was right and she told me, "Of course. What took you so long to get it?" I honestly don't know, but I guess I was not picking up on that particular message Allen was sending. Donna said everyone was cool with Max, Allen's roommate, because they were not his pictures and he seemed to be a nice guy. Someone needed to tell Allen why people, particularly women, were so aloof toward him. She said I should be the one, but I couldn't do it until now. Even a seemingly simple task as decorating your room can give people an idea of who you

> It's important to realize how little things can really matter to others.

are (or aren't), so it's important to realize how little things can really matter to others without your even realizing them.

You see, just because you are a "nice" person who means well and goes through life trying to be good to others does not mean that that is how others actually perceive you. The message you are trying to send (in Allen's case, that he is a good guy and is a friendly person) is not necessarily the message being received by those with whom you come into contact. Take a moment and view the CAMPUS CHARMS on the next page to learn helpful hints on communicating the message you want others to receive.

> The message you are trying to send is not necessarily the message being received.

CAMPUS CHARMS

1. More than ninety percent of all communication is non-verbal. "Who you are speaks so loudly that I do not need to hear what you are saying."

2. Communicate clearly: Speak without mumbling, maintain eye contact, and don't fidget!

3. When speaking, seek feedback. Ask "What do you think?" or "And what about you?" throughout the entire conversation so you do not become a monopolizer.

4. When listening, paraphrase. That is, say "What I hear you saying is this, is that what you mean?" Summarize the message you think the other person is trying to communicate to you.

5. Learn to "read" people. Listen for tone, voice inflections, and watch body language.

6. Continually seek to improve your skills at communication. Great communicators are personally fulfilled and are our society's winners.

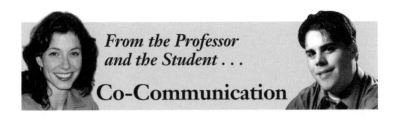

From the Professor and the Student . . .
Co-Communication

EFFECTIVE COMMUNICATION inside and outside the classroom is crucial to getting what you need from your college. Once you learn effective communication strategies to relate to other students, roommates, and your professors, you are ready to reach out and communicate with the rest of your college. Mastering the skill of effective communication is vital to your success not only in college but also in life.

How to Communicate Effectively Inside Your College

1. Go to your campus career center. While there, look up lists of jobs in your chosen major. Talk to the counselors about getting ready for your future. Take advantage of the career center. On many campuses, this place is the hidden secret that can help you land your dream job.

2. Talk to your schedule advisor early in the semester. Don't wait until registration; by the end of the semester, every advisor is busy with other students. Find out who your advisor is, and ask him or her what classes you should take each semester for the next four years. Advisors are there to help; they want you to seek their advice.

3. Talk to juniors and seniors in your chosen major. They may be able to tell you what classes to avoid and what professors are good to have. Some of them might have insight into a campus job that you might be interested in. For example, if you are a journalism major, you probably want to pursue a position with your campus newspaper.

4. Talk to professors in your major. Find out about possible future employment for students who have chosen your major. Also, ask these professors or the departmental assistant about communicating with some former students who have since graduated and have gone on to get jobs. What kinds of jobs did they get? Are they satisfied? These students may have some internship leads for you.

5. Make an appointment with the chair of your major department. Find out from the chair if there are any scholarships available in your major.

6. Go to the financial aid office at your school to learn about scholarships, grants, and work/study jobs that are available. There is so much money out there for college students—all you have to do is look. We also recommend that you go to www.fastweb.com to create a personal profile and launch a comprehensive scholarship search.

7. Join campus organizations and learn how to communicate effectively with your fellow students.

8. Check out campus bulletin boards for information on jobs and clubs you might be interested in. Most bulletins are posted in your school's student union or center, but you should also check out the bulletin boards in the departmental office of your chosen major.

9. Go to the library! Check out the boards there and talk to the librarians.

10. Visit your university's international students center and find out about any study abroad programs they are offering.

How to Communicate Effectively Outside Your College

1. Join community organizations (environmental, social, church, political, or charity organizations) to meet people doing good deeds in your community.

2. Get to know community leaders or the movers and shakers in your area.

3. Find out the names of the editors of your local newspaper. Write an editorial, or offer to send in something you do well, like photography. Although the newspaper may not pay you, it may print what you submit, an accomplishment you can put on your résumé.

4. Communicate with your boss. Find out something about him or her outside the confines of your employment.

5. If your family is local, talk to your parents or friends of your parents. How are they active in the community? What kinds of job openings do they know about?

6. Learn the name of your Congressional representative.

RLU
Reflection
Section
#2

1. What does it mean to be a good communicator?

_____

_____

2. Why are effective e-mail messages so important?

_____

_____

3. What makes a good e-mail message? A bad one? Make two lists.

_____

_____

4. What are some pet peeves of professors? What can you do to shine in the classroom? How about outside the classroom?

_____

_____

5. If you live in a dorm, what should you do if you have a miscommunication with your roommate or Resident Assistant?

_____

_____

6. Why should you go out of your way to meet and communicate with people who are very different from you?

_____

_____

7. How do you gauge your proxemics when talking to someone else? _____

_____

8. What are some things you can do to "charm" your campus listeners during conversations?

_____

_____

9. Where can you go to communicate effectively on campus? Off campus?

_____

_____

CHAPTER 3

THINKING RELATIONSHIPS?

BUILD BRIDGES BY YEAR THREE

Real Life University

ARE YOU READY? From the previous chapter, you will recall the constant reminders of the importance of communication. In this chapter, you will begin to understand the reason for the sense of urgency placed upon communication: Without it you will not be able to initiate or maintain meaningful relationships. Without such meaningful relationships, crucial parts of your college experience will prove to be rather difficult.

If your high school years were anything like ours, you heard over and over again that a big part of college is trying new things and meeting new people, all of which is definitely true. So let's focus on the new people for a bit. We have already established that they are all unique and different, so studied communication is vital if you wish to foster real relationships with people inside your university and in the real world. The first people with whom you are likely to have the opportunity for up-close interaction (unless you are a student athlete or you live at home) are the ones who live in close proximity to you—your residence hall or house community is where you will see, meet, talk to, talk about, like, dislike, fight, make up, and probably go through the process all over again with your closest peers. Always remember to look at the perspective of the other person in a relationship as well as your own, and you will find that many of your interactions with others will prove to be positive ones.

FALL SEMESTER:
From the Student . . .
Michael's Meanings

R ELATIONSHIPS CANNOT be built on poor communication; both parties need to understand the concepts used in the communication. And without the communication, relationships will not succeed. Relationships come and go throughout our lives, but they are much more likely to grow into strong personal bonds if the connection is driven by a dialogue that is both understood and agreed upon by both parties. Throughout college, you will be faced with situations that require good communication skills in order to get through the situation. When poor communication exists, the outcome of the relationship can be drastic.

One of the biggest communication problems I see on campus and hear about from other students is quarrels between roommates. However, miscommunication between roommates oftentimes can be easily eliminated. When I think about all the problems Grant and I had in the beginning of our relationship, I cannot think of more than two times that could not have been prevented if we tried harder to communicate with one other. Sure, there may be some things such as hygiene and bad habits, but most of the other problems that come up can be solved before they even become an issue.

If your roommate goes to sleep early and you stay up late then talk about it—figure out how you can work it out. Perhaps you can go down the hall to the lounge and watch television or nap in a friend's room. If your roommate always has a member of the opposite sex over and you think that you have no privacy at night then you have to tell your roommate how you feel—keeping it a secret will solve nothing.

I had a friend who really disliked his roommate because he never made his bed in the morning. While this reason for disliking him may sound ridiculous to you, it illustrates that even the smallest of things can trigger anger and resentment. Whenever my friend would get mad about the unmade bed, he would immediately run down the hall to my room and tell the guys that were sitting in there about how much he really hated his roommate. Well, eventually what he was telling us got terribly twisted into a false rumor that got back to his roommate. The two guys had a huge falling-out over what was going around and ended up having to go through the hassle of switching roommates. The entire problem could have been prevented if my friend had confronted his roommate about something as simple as making his bed. But instead, because of a lack of communication, the once-small problem got way out of control, and a potential valuable friendship suffered.

> Even the smallest of things can trigger anger and resentment.

The same principle of honesty and candidness applies with all of your relationships in college. It is important to foster those relationships and make sure you are able to keep them. Whether you are on the baseball field, in the theater, at lunch, or just in your dorm room, you have to be an effective communicator to have worthwhile relationships, and relationships are the stepping stones to success in college.

From the moment you step foot on campus for freshmen orientation, you should be thinking about how you can form valuable relationships with those around you. While I recognize that many of us are tempted to make the "Love 101" strategies a top priority, it is crucial to not forget about the professional relationships that need time and development during your college years. Personal relationships are incredibly important and fulfilling, but you also need to cultivate your business relationships for your future success and happiness.

SPRING SEMESTER:
From the Professor . . .
Networking with Nicole

GETTING ALONG with roommates, RAs, class-mates, and even current and former "love interests" is important during your college years, but some of the most relevant relationships you should make are with:

1. Faculty members (professors, lecturers, etc.)

2. Staff (career center workers, advisors, etc.)

3. Administration members (deans, academic vice presidents, etc.)

4. Colleagues (classmates who will work with you on campus projects, community organizations, etc.)

5. Business leaders in the community

How do you build relationships with these people? Contrary to the negative rumors I have heard on and off over the past decade, university faculty and staff members are usually very accessible. Also, you can take classes with professors, so you see them every day. The best way to get to know professors, however, is to work with them outside the walls of the classroom. In most cases, teaching faculty are required to post "office hours," or times when they will be in their offices ready to talk with you or answer any questions you have about the course or, more often than not, anything else you have questions about. Most professors have one office hour for every hour they teach; the fewest number of faculty hours I have seen required at a university is three hours a week.

I am about to tell you the biggest secret about office hours: Hardly any undergraduate students visit their professors during this time. What a mistake! While I understand the reasons why most undergrads choose not to visit their professors—too busy, too intimidated, too awkward to talk to a professor one-on-one—I cannot stress enough the important of trying to get to know at least some if not all of your professors. No, I am not asking you to try to be adopted by your professor's family, but just a few (maybe three or four) visits spread throughout the entire semester will do wonders for your college success. Of course, there are those students who will want to camp out in their professor's office every free minute they have, and you are almost better off never going to a professor's office than being one of these lackey student types. However, to never visit any professor's office robs you of valuable career and networking connections.

What I mean by networking is simply what the word means broken up

The best way to get to know professors is to work with them outside the walls of the classroom.

into smaller words: working the net. The "net," of course, is your school, and the people in the net are the most important contact people (mentioned above) with whom you should form relationships. To "work the net" simply means to spend some of your time with these individuals. This time spent usually starts out with your going into the professor's office and asking a question about a paper, project, or assignment you are working on. The majority of professors are very receptive to students. We became teachers because we want to help you learn and better understand our subject matter areas. Once you ask a question, the talking flows, and you may find you and your professor share some common interest in a topic, issue, or even a hobby. For example, you and your professor may both consider *The Godfather* to be your favorite movie of all time, but you'd never know it without walking into those office hours.

> Hardly any undergraduate students visit their professors during office hours. What a mistake!

In the best-case scenario, your professor may know someone in the industry where you want to work; a positive letter of recommendation from that professor may help you secure a job with his or her colleague's company. For example, the reason Michael and I ended up writing this book together is because he came and visited me during office hours. Although I must be honest with you and say that I was very noncommittal (at best!) the first few times Michael came in and approached me about this book idea, I admired his politeness and persistence, and eventually I agreed to listen to his idea in entirety. Since then, we have formed a valuable relationship that has been beneficial to both of us.

The worst-case scenario of trying to talk to a professor during office hours is that you find that you and your professor don't have much in common. Just remember that at least you have the class in common, so go from there. However, as we pointed out in the communication chapter, you may still want to pursue at least an acquaintance with this professor because you and s/he may realize down the road that you have some common foothold. If not, at least you will have practiced the valuable communication strategy of learning from those people who are most different from you. Remember, if you can't talk to your professor during his or her scheduled office hours because you have a class or another important commitment, many professors agree to see students on a "by appointment" basis and will be happy to meet with you during a scheduled time that

To never visit any professor's office robs you of valuable career and networking connections.

is convenient for both of you. One word of warning, though: If you schedule an individual appointment with a professor, you must make the appointment, and you must be on time. I had a Shakespeare professor who came into our 8:00 A.M. class fuming mad, saying "One word to the wise—if you schedule a 7:00 A.M. appointment with a professor, you better make sure you be there." The professor may have had to travel to campus especially for your visit, so if you miss the appointment, the professor will surely not think too highly of you, and your attempt to network in order to improve your relationship and future college career has actually backfired.

> **Many professors see students on a "by appointment" basis and will be happy to meet with you.**

Faculty members are not the only link to college success, however. Some of the most helpful people on college campuses are staff and/or people in administration. Administrators are often people who were once professors, but who have "moved up" your university's ladder to actually help run the university (marketing, publicity, lawsuits, increasing enrollments, etc.).

Some of the most important administrators are the deans. You can go and visit a dean when you have a question or a problem, or you can just go and meet your deans just so they know how you are. Deans, although very busy, are almost always happy to see you because the students are like customers: Deans like to keep you happy at their university so you don't transfer. Don't take advantage of deans, but do know that they are there to help you. Let's say, for example, that you think you have a professor who is unfairly grading you, or you are having problems transferring credits from another school and your advisor is unsure—a dean will almost always step in and help you. However, a dean is not going to come to you; you have to make an appointment with the dean's office.

Administrators are officially part of the staff (non-teaching) aspect of universities, but there are plenty of other staff people around who are not in administration—janitors, landscapers, police officers, etc. The police will help you when you lock your keys in your car or get a flat tire, so it sure helps to not be on their bad side; you will also be wise to be on good terms with the janitorial staff. I can't tell you the number of times a janitor unlocked a building when I needed to have a campus organization meeting; or how about the landscaper who used his truck to carry my bicycle all the way to my dorm when some obsessive ex-boy-

If you schedule an appointment, you must make the appointment, and you must be on time.

friend decided to slash my tires? Although you may have your personal reasons for not wanting to befriend staff members, you should always strive not to be snobbish. At the very least, learn the names of staff members who work in the buildings you frequent the most (the cafeteria, student center, classroom buildings when you attend classes in your major, or the recreational center).

Nicole's Nine Networking Tips:

E*veryone counts.* Make eye contact with everyone—especially faculty, staff, and administrators—while walking around your own RLU campus. Smile when you make eye contact; you may eventually have a class or work with a faculty member you made eye contact with, and s/he will remember you positively.

T*hink ahead*: Don't wait until your senior year to start developing relationships with university employees. Start now so you can build sincere, meaningful, and helpful connections.

W*ork on your networking whenever you can.* If you get to class early and you are the only one there with your professor, strike up a simple conversation (weather/campus politics/the economy) or ask a question or two about an upcoming assignment or midterm. Some professors go to class early because they want to talk to students to see if you need help, and get to know you. If you're alone with a staff or administration member, say hello and start up a conversation.

Organize your schedule so you have some time to get to know people. If you take only night classes that you have to run to get to on time from work, and then you leave right after class is over, you won't have allowed yourself any valuable time to invest in your relationship with your professor, an investment that may ultimate help you have a more successful future.

Remember to say thank you! If a janitor or librarian opens a building for you early, look the person directly in the eye and say THANK YOU with a big smile. Please also remember to send personal, handwritten thank-you notes when people do favors for you (write you a letter of recommendation, invite you to dinner, allow you to drop a class after the drop deadline, etc.). E-mail thank-yous are appropriate only for smaller deeds, such as when a professor gives you advice on a paper or assignment, or a staff member gives you directions to a campus building, etc.

Kill them with kindness. People love happy people, and studies show that people view happy individuals as more skilled, self confident, and in control of their own lives.

Inquire about the "right" places to network. Go to your campus career center, and talk to a career counselor about the kinds of organizations you should be joining, internships you should be trying to get, etc.

Notice your e-mail and paper postings for campus events around campus. You can learn about the best jobs and campus networking opportunities that way. Sometimes, even the postings that don't seem to have networking potential can work in your favor. For example, I once received a mass mailing (an e-mail posting sent to everyone in my department) from my department director, asking us about the number of engineering students in our classes. When I e-mailed him back to find out more about it, we started an e-mail conversation about a project of having new sections of English specifically for engineering students. It turned out he was too busy and didn't have time to organize the new classes and wondered would I be interested in being the Communications Consultant and Departmental Liaison between the two departments? If I had not pursued that e-mail communication, I would have missed out on a valuable position that gave me networking experience.

Give yourself to charity. Working with campus and community volunteer groups will provide you with crucial connections to social, political, and industry leaders who will remember you when it comes time to get a job in your community.

For many of you, however, networking on campus will mean joining campus politics, clubs, or social organizations, such as fraternities or sororities. If you're smart, you'll constantly be on the lookout for volunteer work, jobs, internships, or travel opportunities in your areas of interest (pull out your **Life-Jacket List** from chapter 1). The "lookout" consists of flyers posted around campus, the campus newspaper, and bulletin boards in the career center or student union, or e-mails you receive on your student account. (Many college departments send mass e-mails to all students in their discipline; other universities actually send mass e-mailings to all students in an attempt to reach you and save some money on snail mail costs.) Getting involved in campus activities is a wonderful way to make new friends; it is also a résumé builder. The more you become involved, the more people you come in contact with and the better your chances of meeting someone who is really going to help you get a job or will know someone who knows someone who has an opening. Statistics show that almost ninety percent of jobs are gotten by *who* you know (your network of contacts) not *what* you know (your GPA). That's not to say that what you know isn't important because it is.

So, go to class, but make sure to attend and get involved in a variety of activities outside the classroom as well.

So far, I have spent a lot time in my half of this chapter talking about the importance of building relationships through effective communication and networking. College students also need to know about the "chain of command"—the hierarchy of staff, faculty, and administrators at universities—because knowing the chain of command in business (and college is BIG business) will help you avoid communication blunders. For example, if you have a complaint about your course grade in college, where do you go first? The professor, of course. If you go above the professor's head (department head, chair, or dean) *before* talking to the professor, you may find yourself in some pretty hot water. The rule of thumb is that when you have a complaint, you follow the chain of command, and you carefully document everything about your communication processes with the parties involved. If your professor won't change your grade and you feel your complaint is justifiable and provable, then you can start going "up the chain" of people in power. However, if you fail to go to your professor (or whoever is the person

> **!** Almost ninety percent of jobs are gotten by who you know, not what you know.

with whom you are directly communicating) first, you may find your grade will never get changed because you did not follow the chain of command. Moreover, professors—believe it or not—do talk to one another, and the last thing you need in college is a professor who tells all the other faculty members what a troublemaker you are.

RLU Requirement #3 **Know the communication "chain of command" at your university.**

Always approach the person with whom you are having a communication problem first; talk with his or her supervisor after you have confronted your problem communicator.

Gradually go up the college ladder of professional, rung by rung, until your communication dilemma is solved.

RLU
Reflection
Section

#3

Here is a glossary of campus terms you need to know to succeed in RLU:

Academic Probation: A formal warning to a student that his or her work is not meeting the requirements of the institution. In most cases, a student cannot be on academic probation for more than one semester.

Add/Drop: Time period in which a student may add a specific class to his or her schedule or drop a class from his or her schedule.

Advisor: A faculty member who is assigned to a student to help them determine their classes and other academic concerns.

Application Process: Process a student goes through in order to formally request admission into a specific university or college.

Associate's Degree: A degree received after the completion of a two-year program.

Audit: Registration in a class for knowledge purposes only. A student is given no academic credit when he or she does a course audit.

Bachelor's Degree: Degree received after the completion of undergraduate studies—usually one hundred twenty-eight hours.

Core Classes: Classes that must be taken in order for a student to receive a degree from the institution.

Credit: The amount of hours a student receives for completing a specific course. This is determined by the number of hours a student spends in the classroom.

Dean: The highest position within a department or school division.

Dean's List: An award given to students for academic achievement.

Degree: The academic title given to a student after he or she completes the necessary courses in their field of study.

Elective: A course that is optional and does not fit into a student's specific discipline.

Fee: Money charged to a student for services received. Usually fees are assessed for labs and courses that require out-of-the-ordinary materials.

Financial Aid: Money given to a student by the institution, government, or private foundations in order to assist in making college affordable to the student.

Independent Study: A course taken by a student under direct supervision of a professor but with no classroom time.

Internship: Work completed by a student that directly relates to his or her major. Oftentimes academic credit is given for completed internships.

Major: A specialized field of study in which a student chooses to get a degree.

Master's Degree: A degree given to a student upon the completion of graduate school.

Office Hours: Time set aside by a professor to assist students.

Prerequisite: Class that is mandatory before a student can move on to a more-advanced level course.

Resident Advisor: Person who enforces the rules and regulations in the dormitories and assists students with any problems they may have.

Resident Director: Person who is in charge of a dormitory; Resident Advisor's boss.

Remedial Course: A course that is needed to bring a student to the collegiate level in areas of study such as math, reading, and writing.

Scholarship: Money given to a student to assist with the cost of his or her education. Scholarships do not have to be paid back.

Student Housing: Department in charge of on-campus living. Usually offers residence halls and apartments.

Syllabus: A synopsis of what is expected from the student for a specific course; also outlines important dates and assignments.

Transcript: An official record of a student's educational progress in the area of academics.

Work Study: On-campus jobs offered to students.

CHAPTER 4

FOCUSING ON THE FUTURE

LEAD BY YEAR FOUR

Real Life University

WE HAVE TALKED about the importance of your making the decisions necessary to be successful in college. Successful people make it because they do allow themselves to admit and learn from their mistakes. Winning college students also allow themselves to ask for help when they need it (especially when it seems hard to ask), try to learn from their mishaps, and take great joy in their achievements. However, even the best students during and after college need encouragement and must rely on others. Yes, you as a successful student will have your low points too, but what you need to remember always is to trust in yourself and to lean on others when you need to.

One of the greatest downfalls of college students today is they expect others to believe in them before they believe in themselves. Many people out there will do all they can to hinder your success because they are envious. You have to make a conscious effort to not let those people hurt you. We, much like many of you, have encountered many obstacles when we decided to take the next step on to college. There were those people who said to Michael, "You know, college isn't for everyone. It is okay if you just go into the work force and get a job" and who said to Nicole, "Good grades are all you need to be successful in life." The words spoken by those people in our lives still linger to this day, but only in the sense that we both knew we could do better or differently than what others told us.

> College students expect others to believe in them before they believe in themsleves.

In order to be successful in college, be sure to give yourself the chance to *dream*:

Develop a plan.

Recognize your potential.

Explore your options.

Activate your plan.

Make it happen (and maintain a positive attitude).

FALL SEMESTER:
From the Student . . .

Making Michael

I WILL BE the first one to admit that I was a very average, and at times, a below-average student in high school. My grades never climbed above a C average, and my test scores ranked among the lowest in my class. Granted, I was very ill for awhile and missed lots of class because of extensive hospital stays out of state, and I was diagnosed with two learning disabilities. For most of my high school career, I attended what I thought was the "best school" in New Orleans. Then, after I got back from the hospital in Denver, I decided that I was going to turn my life around so I transferred schools. During the first semester of my junior year, I enrolled at my first school's biggest rival. I was determined to better my grades—it suddenly became clear to me that if I didn't, there was no way I was going to even have the chance to go to college, learning disability or no learning disability.

While the majority of the people in my life assured me that I was just not "school material," this one man stood by my side and actually changed my life. He was one of those teachers who just loved what he did; his passion for teaching echoed through the room day after day. The first day I met Mr. Barouse, he assured me that I was going to be in all the same classes as the rest of the students at the school, and I was going to be treated like a "normal" student and not one with a learning disability.

Mr. Barouse taught me how to turn my disabilities into my strongest assets. Every day I spent two hours in his classroom working on math and science. When I would get a problem right he made me feel as if I were the smartest guy in the world. It was because of his positive influence in my life that I was able to get a B average in school for the first time ever. Instead of thinking that taking Ritalin was a hassle, I began to think it was a help. He helped me realize that just because I am dyslexic and ADHD did not mean that I could not succeed in school. There is no doubt in my mind that this man is one of the main reasons I am a successful student—both inside and outside the classroom—today. Every time I get grades at midterm and semester breaks, I always call him and brag about them to him. He is just as happy as I am.

If your high school experience was anything like the experience of most students, then you probably had that one teacher who just dedicated his or her life to the classroom. The greatest thing this awesome teacher did for me was to get me to believe in myself. After I was able to do that, there was nothing in my way. I overcame severe dyslexia, ADHD, and COPD like it was nothing. Missing school when I was sick was not as big of a deal as it used to be because I knew how to catch up more easily. My stress level dramatically decreased and my self-confidence skyrocketed. In my short time as a student of Mr. Barouse's, I began to understand what success felt like. He truly believed in me, and because of his guidance and encouragement, I was prepared for college.

Once I started college, I again found myself somewhat stereotyped, and my first college courses were LD, or Learning Disabled, and I took them the summer before I started college because they were "special" classes. I didn't feel special; I felt rather stupid in fact. I had already been a motivational speaker to thousands of high school students, and here I was, again, in remedial classes. However, I was determined not to let those classes get to me. Instead, I pressed on and made sure that those around me realized that I could accomplish anything I wanted to accomplish if I put my mind to it. By the time the end of the summer came, I think I proved my point! I completed my classes with a straight-A average—one of only two members of the program to do so. Additionally, I was one step ahead of the rest of the incoming freshmen because I had already begun to form relationships with professors and administrators.

I never imagined transferring high schools would change my life as much as it did. The professors that taught me those remedial classes gave me hope for my future. They both made me realize just how easy it is to succeed if you really want to. It is unfortunate that not all professors are as sincere and dedicated as those two are. You have to learn to get past those who aren't. In the meantime, thank those who have helped you.

During freshman orientation at my college, one of the leaders was asked the question, "What is the first thing I should do before classes start?" His reply was incredible. He said, "You should write a note to your high school teachers who encouraged you to come to college. Those teachers are probably a big reason you are here about to start a new chapter in your life." I was surprised to find out that almost all of my orientation group valued this leader's suggestion and carried it out. You should do the same: Make a list below of any teacher or coach or mentor who has helped you believe in yourself. Then, send a handwritten thank-you note to all the individuals, letting them know just much they have positively influenced your life.

List of People I Want to Thank

1. _____

2. _____

3. _____

4. _____

5. _____

College certainly is a time for you to grow, a time for you to learn who you are, and a time for you to find your beliefs. If you give yourself the chance to really explore the wonderful word that college offers, there is no doubt that you will benefit from it. Yes, there are going to be those out there who are going to try to bring you down and tell you that "you are not college material," and there will be occasions that you will feel like a failure, but you have to believe in yourself. It simply does not matter what others think . . . you can do what you dream you can do. Believe me, if a former special-ed kid can get A's, serve on student government, be a professional speaker, organize a charity event, and write a book with his professor, I promise you that you can do whatever you set your mind to.

It simply does not matter what others think.

No one ever travels the road of real life, however, without obstacles, and you will encounter some. Your ability to handle these rough spots can make or break you. Remember, almost every mistake can be remedied with time and patience. The most important thing you need to do in the meantime is forgive yourself and move on. The most successful people make lots of mistakes because they are go-getters; and you can turn every single mishap in your life into a positive influence if you choose.

SPRING SEMESTER:
From the Professor . . .

Knowing Nicole

BEING TOLD you can't do something has to be one of the worst feelings in the world. I can't imagine what Michael or what any person would be thinking when told that "they couldn't make it" in life, in college, etc. No one can tell you whether or not you're going to make it; you make that decision all on your own. Your ability to know yourself and believe in yourself as a successful individual and to communicate well and form valuable relationships with others depends only on you. I have seen thousands of students in my teaching career accomplish tasks because they simply believed they could, and no one was going to tell them otherwise.

The road to RLU is not always an easy one; however, and you must forgive yourself for the mistakes you make. Unlike Michael, I was told by my teachers and everyone else what a gifted student I was, but the problem was that I didn't believe in myself as a student or as a person. Always looking for the easy way out, I took meaningless courses and tried

> No one can tell you whether or not you're going to make it; you make that decision all on your own.

to get by doing as little work as possible. I wish I could justify this lackadaisical (read: Apathy!) attitude toward school with a rendition of a busy schedule in extracurricular activities, but to be honest, I really wasn't that busy—just insecure and afraid—afraid of the challenge, afraid someone might tell me I was average or just didn't measure up, etc. In many ways, Michael and I had opposite school experiences: Things were difficult for Michael, so he had to rise to the task, but things were so easy for me grade-wise that I, like many students who do not feel challenged by school, tried to cut corners.

Eventually my attitude caught up with me, and my 4.0 high school grade point average began slipping. By the time I entered college, I was in such full-fledged denial about my social insecurities and communication problems that I gave up on school. I earned a 1.5 GPA at the end of my fall semester during my freshman year and was put on probation. Eventually the mercy of a dean who dropped a five-credit F for me brought my GPA up to a 2.5, but life was still in the valley.

We all make mistakes. I had skipped class, failed tests, and was put on school probation. As a "good kid" I thought my life was over, and that I might as well not even finish college. I did finish and managed to graduate on the dean's list, but I was so out of touch with what was important in real life that all I managed to do was class work. We don't want you to waste your college years trying to figure out who you are; decide beforehand (or early enough in your college career for it to matter) what your likes and dislikes are, and go from there. The exercises and examples on communication, relationships, and networking will help you make the necessary connections needed to bring you personal satisfaction and future success. They helped me—just about four years after college and almost too late.

You have a chance now to make a big difference in your own life by becoming a successful college student. One of my students this semester, Tara, recently asked me to answer some interview questions about college. A transcript of the interview is below; I hope the answers will provide a window into one example of college professor/student interaction outside the classroom. I also hope it will help you not to make some common mistakes that college students make.

TM: Where did you attend undergraduate school and what are some of the things you recall about your first year in college?

NA: I went to a very large state school. Although I went to college in my hometown, I found my first year in a college of forty-seven thousand students to be very lonely. My classes were big, swim practice and my job were tough, and my roommate and I had nothing in common. I was a very insecure seventeen-year-old thrust into this big, impersonal place, and I didn't do very well. I actually failed out of my first semester of college.

TM: What led to your decision to become a university professor?

NA: Two main reasons:

1. I "fell" into the profession—after college I could not get a decent job (I sold knives door to door), so I decided to go on to graduate school because my grades were very good. English was my major in college, so I immediately went on to the master's level in English, and I began teaching college at twenty-one to support myself. More education lead to more education, and now I have been a teacher for the past decade.

2. My subject matter just came easy to me. Sometimes, you gravitate toward what you do well, even if you don't at the time understand why you're good at it.

TM: How do you rate the relative importance of teaching and research?

NA: Teaching is my number-one priority. The value

of the hundreds of students I've taught and the thousands I have yet to teach is more important to me than any research article. I do try to research, present, and publish, but only to the extent that the research somehow helps me or others become better teachers.

TM: To what extent do you believe faculty should be involved with students outside the classroom?

NA: I think faculty members should mentor students by advising them, serving on committees, chairing an honors program, etc. Building professional relationships with faculty members will help you succeed in college.

TM: What do you consider to be the most important attributes of an ideal college student?

NA: College students should have respect for themselves, the professor, and other students. They should also be hard-working and independent thinkers; students who are go-getters and mark their own paths are the most successful in college. Moreover, I wish college students were more concerned with learning and growing as individuals and less obsessed with grades; unless you really plan to go to graduate, medical, or law school, not many employers care about your 3.821908746 GPA.

TM: What advice can you give me as a freshman that will help me succeed?

NA: Doing the above, plus getting *very involved* in the right campus and community organizations. "Right" just means right for you, and your field, major, future career, etc. Don't waste time in a dead-end job that will get you nowhere later in life; instead, do an internship in your major, travel abroad, volunteer for Habitat for Humanity, etc. Four years from now, employers are going to ask you in job interviews about what you did in college *outside* the classroom. Of course, if you're just in college to get your MRS degree (a.k.a. meet a husband), then go ahead and be Miss Social Bunny, but don't ruin a good (and expensive!) education if you don't have to. You might regret it later.

Students also need to network better with the faculty and staff. I know everyone is busy with their own lives, but you need to get to know faculty and staff members so that they can recommend you for a job, a scholarship, an internship, etc. Faculty and staff hear a lot about opportunities for your future, and you as a student will miss out if you don't (1) build a connection with faculty and staff and (2) keep contact with these individuals during and after your college career. Just send an e-mail once in awhile or stop by their offices to let them know how you're doing.

Finally, go to the Campus Career Center as a freshman or, at the very latest, a sophomore, and find out what kinds of jobs are available in your major. You'd be surprised how quickly you'll want to change your major when you find out your chances and desires for certain types of employment. It would be better if you knew this information *now*, right? Again, don't say you don't have time—this is your future here. What's more important than that? The Career Center can also get you started on how to build a good résumé—you know, volunteering, serving on campus organizations, etc.

A S WE DISCUSSED in the introduction, your four or five years in college can be compared to preparing for a job interview. Throughout this book, we have covered the components necessary for college or your "four-year college job interview." If you have a good résumé, excellent communication skills, cultivated relationships, and a positive outlook on life, you have a great chance to be successful in your quest. Always be cognizant of the fact that even the simplest things will play an integral role in your success: your attire, your attitude, your actions, and most of all, your ability to believe in yourself.

APPENDIX

EXTRACURRICULARS

Real Life University

ALTHOUGH YOU and only you can determine your college success, a few odds and ends can help you along the way. Think of these "extracurriculars" as the nice clothes and briefcase you'll need to ace that important job interview. . . .

1. Accept Diversity! A lot of people out there in the college world are not going to look like you, act like you, or think like you, but if you give them a chance they may become your best friends. You will be amazed by what you can learn from members of another religion, culture, or country.

2. Ask Questions! There is no shame in asking questions. Asking questions is the main reason you are in class—to learn. If you have a question and you don't ask it, then you are not being fair to yourself.

3. Avoid Credit Card Death. Don't fall for those brochures in the student center that offer you "low interest for life!" Chances are, it's not true. There usually is some loophole in the paperwork that you don't know about. One of the biggest financial problems among college students is the credit card debt they accrue. If you absolutely have to have one, then be smart and responsible with it. Don't forget that what you charge you have to pay for—now or later!

4. Do Your Homework! Many times professors will put homework on their syllabus and never talk about it again. After about the third class, when you realize that the professor is not going to pick it up, it will seem very tempting to just ignore it and not do it. Professors do not waste their time and pick this work out for no reason. Homework is designed to help you understand the material and oftentimes triggers questions. Do it and do it right!

5. Explore Courses! Don't just take classes that are in your field. There is no shame in taking a geology class if you are a history major. Who knows, you may find out that you absolutely love geology. College is about becoming a broad, well-rounded individual, so take advantage of that opportunity.

6. Find a Charity! Give part of yourself to volunteer or charity work because not only is it good for your résumé, but it also makes you feel good to help others.

7. Get a Job! Jobs teach responsibility and time

management. Many colleges have positions on campus for students who are interested in them, which means if you don't have a car, you can still have a job. Campus jobs are also a great way to make some extra cash for the weekends.

8. Ignore Homesickness! Avoid the temptation to go home every weekend; cut the apron strings as soon as you get to college.

9. Join a Club! There is a lot to be said about getting involved—it really enhances your experience in college. But don't join the club for the wrong reason. If you are a member, make sure when you leave, the club will benefit from what you did for it while you were there.

10. Keep a Journal! These are, after all, the best years of your life.

11. Keep Things in Perspective. Try to remember that the future is exciting, not terrifying. Every one of us has down times, but the students who make it learn to climb out of the valleys. Who knows what will happen when tomorrow comes?

12. Know Your Classmates! It is always a good idea to get the phone numbers and e-mail addresses of a few classmates that you can call if you have any questions about your notes or the textbook. These study buddies are especially helpful during midterms and finals.

13. Plan Photo Ops! These are going to be some of the best years of your life. You don't want to just have to use your mind to remember the good times. Bring a camera with you everywhere and take a few pictures—you don't want to have to rely on your friends to give you doubles.

14. Carry Quarters. Don't leave home with out 'em! You are guaranteed to have problems if you don't have quarters. They will save your life! You need them for everything from that midnight snack out of the vending machine, to copying research in the library, to making a call on a pay phone, to doing your laundry.

15. Schedule Smart! When it comes time for you to pick your classes, do it as early as possible. Remember that classes fill up quickly, so you don't want to be left with nothing. Another thing to remember when it's time to schedule: Give yourself some time between classes. Don't take four classes back to back on Monday, Wednesday, and Friday because you won't have time to eat, go to the bathroom, or run across campus to make it on time to your next class.

16. Start From Day One! From the moment you receive your syllabus for a particular class, be sure you do everything required of you—and do it *on time!* Get a daily planner, and write down the important dates for your class. If you act responsibly from day one, you set a pattern of "planning ahead" that you should continue to do so all semester.

17. Start Strong! If you bear down from the beginning, then you don't have to worry about bringing your D to an A at finals—a grade change that probably won't ever happen. It is very easy to bring your grades down but *terribly* hard to bring them up.

18. Stay Positive! There are going to be many times when you are going to just feel like you want to quit and the world is against you. Don't worry—every college student hits that point at one time or another. Just be sure you maintain your composure and stay positive. Attitude is everything! Know your strengths and change your weaknesses, and learn from both. Being in college means you are constantly moving forward— you're always progressing toward a goal.

19. Find a Study Place! It is very difficult to get studying done in your dorm room. There are so many distractions that hinder your concentration. If you want to cut back on the time it takes to you to get your work done, find somewhere to go that is away from everything, like the library. Find the atmosphere that suits you—lots of students like coffee, so they spend time at one of those bookstores that have the little coffee shops inside. And **leave your cell phone, pager, and instant messenger off!**

20. Make Study Time! From the start of the semester, set aside a specific time each day to study for your classes. Many professors say that for every hour you spend in class, you should study for two hours. Mathematically, that means if you have fifteen hours in the classroom every week, then you should study for thirty. This fact is not meant to scare you—it's meant to make you aware of the workload that is ahead of you. You don't necessarily have to study thirty hours a week to make good grades, but what you have to do is study enough to be prepared. You can use "waiting time"—waiting for a ride to pick you up, waiting for a class to start, etc.—to study or fill out your daily planner. Five minutes here, ten minutes there add up.

21. Think Smaller is Better! If you have the choice of whether or not to take a small class or a large class, take the small one. The environment is better, and you have much more of an opportunity to interact with the professor and the students in the class. Ultimately, this interpersonal connection may help bring your grade way up.

22. Use the Library! It is there for a reason, and your tuition helps pay for it. It has an abundant amount of resources for you to take advantage of. The librarians really want to help you out.

23. Use Your Meal Plan! You paid for one, so use it! Don't go out to eat every day because it's not good for your stomach or your wallet. The cafeteria is a great place to meet new friends and hang out, so take advantage of it.

24. Walk to Class! When you walk to your classes, it gives you the opportunity to meet and greet people along the way. Also, it's a great way to work off the "freshman fifteen."

25. Write a Résumé! Create a résumé and constantly update it; it's hard to recall things a week, semester, or year later.

CONGRATULATIONS! You have successfully completed RLU. You can now look forward to a life of success, personal fulfillment, and happiness!

Share the lessons you've learned

Do you have a lesson about Real Life University that you would like the rest of the world to read about? It could be a memory from high school, college, or just everyday life. If so, visit www.reallifeuniversity.com and submit your own original poem, story, quote, or advice for your chance to be published in the next book in our *Real Life University* series.

Michael McMyne

As one of the youngest professional speakers in the nation, Michael McMyne has brought excitement, energy, and enthusiasm to audiences all over the country. His humorous and powerful messages have challenged students and business people alike to rise to the challenges of life. For more information about how Michael can help your school, company, or organization, contact:

McMyne & Associates
The Newpark Building
2901 North Causeway Blvd.
Suite 202
Metairie LA 70002-4838

888/833-4375

www.reallifeuniversity.com
michael@reallifeuniversity.com